JRuby Cookbook™

D1470567

Justin Edelson and Henry Liu

O'REILLY®

Beijing · Cambridge · Farnham · Köln · Sebastopol · Taipei · Tokyo

JRuby Cookbook™

by Justin Edelson and Henry Liu

Published by O'Reilly Media, Inc., 1005 Gravenstein Highway North, Sebastopol, CA 95472.

O'Reilly books may be purchased for educational, business, or sales promotional use. Online editions are also available for most titles (*http://safari.oreilly.com*). For more information, contact our corporate/institutional sales department: 800-998-9938 or *corporate@oreilly.com*.

Editor: Mike Loukides

Production Editor: Sarah Schneider

Copyeditor: Colleen Gorman

Proofreader: Kiel Van Horn

Indexer: Ellen Troutman Zaig

Cover Designer: Karen Montgomery

Interior Designer: David Futato

Illustrator: Jessamyn Read

Printing History:

November 2008:   First Edition.

ISBN: 978-0-596-51980-3

[M]

1225300397

Table of Contents

Preface

*JRuby is just Ruby taking advantage of Java's VM;
taking the suck out of Java and putting some extra
awesome into Ruby.*

—Charles Nutter, JRuby project lead
Twitter, August 7, 2008

And with that quote, Charles Nutter summarizes the two forces that have recently brought attention to the JRuby project: the recognition that Java provides a powerful platform that can be used by languages other than Java, and the increase in interest in the Ruby programming language. In the recipes ahead, we will explore a wide variety of usage scenarios for JRuby. In Charles's terms, some recipes are about taking the suck out of Java, some are about putting some extra awesome into Ruby, and some are about both.

Audience

To fully leverage JRuby, you must be able to move freely between the Java and Ruby domains. In writing the JRuby Cookbook, we had in mind a reader with some understanding of both languages, possibly with a better understanding of one or the other. As a result, you won't find a lot of basic introductory material, save for the first chapter where we illustrate the areas where Ruby and Java are similar as well as where they differ.

Our overall approach is that the purpose of the recipes in this book is not to educate you on some preexisting Java or Ruby capability, but instead to explain how to use JRuby within the context of, or as an enhancement to, these existing capabilities. For example, the recipes in the JRuby on Rails chapter are written for someone who has already created a (working) Rails application.

Organization

Chapter 1, *Getting Started*

This chapter starts off with a brief introduction to JRuby before stepping through a number of basic usages of JRuby, including how to use the RubyGems package management system and how to interact with Java code from Ruby code. The package concludes with a number of recipes about setting up various integrated development environments (IDEs) for working with JRuby.

Chapter 2, *JRuby on Rails*

This chapter is focused on a variety of scenarios for deploying Ruby on Rails applications using JRuby.

Chapter 3, *Java Integration*

This chapter starts with several recipes about invoking Ruby code from Java code and then continues into recipes describing the usage of popular Java libraries such as Java Native Access (JNA) and Jakarta Commons Logging from Ruby.

Chapter 4, *Enterprise Java*

The recipes in this chapter are all about using JRuby with enterprise Java frameworks such as JMS, JNDI, EJB, Spring, and Hibernate.

Chapter 5, *User Interface and Graphics*

This chapter describes a number of JRuby-based frameworks that facilitate the creation of user interfaces. It also includes recipes about image manipulation, applets, and desktop integration.

Chapter 6, *Build Tools*

The recipes in this chapter are focused on using JRuby to enhance the build process of your Java project. Ant and Maven, the two most popular Java-based build tools, both have several different ways that JRuby can be used. There are also recipes about the JRuby-specific build tools Raven and Buildr.

Chapter 7, *Testing*

The focus of this chapter is on JtestR, a package that includes JRuby and a variety of popular Ruby testing tools. Through the recipes in this chapter, you will learn how to write Ruby-based tests of Java code.

Chapter 8, *The JRuby Community*

This final chapter includes a few recipes about effectively participating in the JRuby community.

Conventions Used in This Book

This book uses the following typographic conventions:

Italic

Used for example URLs, names of directories and files, options, and occasionally for emphasis.

`Constant width`

> Used for program listings. Also used within paragraphs to refer to program elements such as namespaces, classes, and method names.

`Constant width italic`

> Indicates text that should be replaced with user-supplied values.

 This icon indicates a tip, suggestion, or general note.

 This icon indicates a warning or caution.

Using Code Examples

This book is here to help you get your job done. In general, you may use the code in this book in your programs and documentation. You do not need to contact us for permission unless you're reproducing a significant portion of the code. For example, writing a program that uses several chunks of code from this book does not require permission. Selling or distributing a CD-ROM of examples from O'Reilly books *does* require permission. Answering a question by citing this book and quoting example code does not require permission. Incorporating a significant amount of example code from this book into your product's documentation *does* require permission.

We appreciate, but do not require, attribution. An attribution usually includes the title, author, publisher, and ISBN. For example: "*JRuby Cookbook*, by Justin Edelson and Henry Liu. Copyright 2009 Justin Edelson and Henry Liu, 978-0-596-51980-3."

If you feel your use of code examples falls outside fair use or the permission given above, feel free to contact us at *permissions@oreilly.com*.

Safari® Books Online

 When you see a Safari® Books Online icon on the cover of your favorite technology book, that means the book is available online through the O'Reilly Network Safari Bookshelf.

Safari offers a solution that's better than e-books. It's a virtual library that lets you easily search thousands of top tech books, cut and paste code samples, download chapters, and find quick answers when you need the most accurate, current information. Try it for free at *http://safari.oreilly.com*.

Comments and Questions

We at O'Reilly have tested and verified the information in this book to the best of our ability, but mistakes and oversights do occur. Please let us know about errors you may find, as well as your suggestions for future editions, by writing to:

O'Reilly Media, Inc.
1005 Gravenstein Highway North
Sebastopol, CA 95472
800-998-9938 (in the U.S. or Canada)
707-829-0515 (international or local)
707-829-0104 (fax)

To ask technical questions or comment on the book, send email to:

bookquestions@oreilly.com

We have a website for this book where examples, errata, and any plans for future editions are listed. You can access this site at:

http://www.oreilly.com/catalog/9780596519803

For more information about this book and others, see the O'Reilly website:

http://www.oreilly.com

Acknowledgments

Thanks to the O'Reilly staff, especially our editor Mike Loukides and copyeditor Colleen Gorman. Thanks to Steven Shingler for his contribution to Chapter 4. And thanks to all who reviewed this book including Juan Pablo Tarquino, John Purcell, and David Koontz.

This book simply would not and could not exist without the tireless efforts of the whole JRuby project team, including Charles Nutter, Thomas Enebo, Nick Sieger, and Ola Bini. Thanks also to Sun and ThoughtWorks for their ongoing support of JRuby. The JRuby project is hosted by The Codehaus; thanks as well to Bob McWhirter for his work there.

We both would like to thank Nick Rockwell for his ongoing encouragement and enthusiasm.

Justin Edelson

This book wouldn't have happened without the love and support of my wonderful wife, Elizabeth. Special thanks to my sons: Owen, who typed his name all by himself, and Benjamin, who can't yet.

Thanks to my team at MTV Networks: Michael Benoit, Keith Griffin, Ramesh Nutha-lapati, Ilya Reznikov, Chris Sindel, Jeff Yemin, and Jun Zhou, for all their hard work. Thanks also to Warren Habib for his support.

Henry Liu

Thanks to my friend Jon Baer for inviting me to my first Ruby meeting and being a great collaborator throughout the years. I'm grateful to Francis Hwang, Matt Pelletier, Sebastian Delmont, Trotter Cashion, and all the members of the NYC Ruby group. They taught me Ruby and Rails by answering all my newbie questions, and it was their passion and enthusiasm for the technology that motivated me to dig deeper. Thanks to all my colleagues at MTV Networks and specifically Mark Ache, Luke Murphy, and Steve Azueta for their continued support. Most of all, thanks to my family and my partner, Naomi; without her, none of this would be possible.

## CHAPTER 1

Getting Started

1.0 Introduction

JRuby is an open source implementation of the Ruby programming language for the Java Virtual Machine (JVM). It allows Ruby applications to be run within a Java Virtual Machine and interface with libraries written in either Java or Ruby. Although the JRuby project was initiated in 2001, interest in JRuby has grown significantly over the last few years, reflecting an overall growth in interest in Ruby sparked by the success of the Ruby on Rails framework. Sun has contributed to JRuby's success by employing members of the core development team and providing support for JRuby in the NetBeans development environment, among other efforts. The website for the JRuby project is currently *http://www.jruby.org*.

Ruby

Ruby is a dynamic object-oriented programming language created by Yukihiro Matsumoto, known by the nickname Matz, in the mid-1990s. Ruby follows a style of versioning similar to the Linux kernel, where an even minor version number indicates a stable release and an odd minor version number indicates a development release. As a result, there are two *current* versions of Ruby: 1.8.6, released in March 2007, is the current stable release, and 1.9.0, released in December 2007, is the current development release. The standard Ruby interpreter* is written in C. There are several alternate implementations of the interpreter, including JRuby, IronRuby (for Microsoft's .NET framework), and Rubinius. Ruby does not have a formal language specification; however, one is being developed through the wiki at *http://spec.ruby-doc.org*.

As an object-orientated language, many of the underlying concepts of Ruby will be familiar to Java developers, even if the syntax is not. The biggest exception to this is Ruby's support for *blocks*. In Ruby, a block is a grouping of code that gets passed to a method call. The receiving method can invoke the block any number of times and can pass parameters to the block. Support for a similar type of element, a *closure*, is being

---

* Usually referred to as Matz's Ruby Interpreter (MRI).

contemplated for inclusion in Java 7; there are several competing proposals and it is unclear which proposal, if any, will be adopted. Example 1-1 contains a simple Ruby class demonstrating the two ways of defining a block in Ruby. The former syntax, using braces, is typically used to create a block for a single statement. The latter syntax, using the do and end keywords, is typically used for multistatement blocks.

Example 1-1. Introduction to Ruby blocks

```ruby
class HelloWorldSayer
    def hello_world
        yield "Hello"
        yield "World"
        yield "from Ruby"
    end
end

sayer = HelloWorldSayer.new
sayer.hello_world { |message| puts message.swapcase }

# or

sayer.hello_world do |it|
    puts it.swapcase
end
```

 The Ruby yield function transfers control to the block argument.

This isn't to suggest that blocks are the only substantial difference between Ruby and Java, but it is certainly one of the most significant, as block usage is so prevalent within typical Ruby code. For example, outputting the list of numbers between 1 and 10 in Java would look something like the code in Example 1-2. The corresponding Ruby code is shown in Example 1-3.

Example 1-2. Loop in Java

```java
for (int i = 1; i <= 10; i++) {
    System.out.println(i);
}
```

Example 1-3. Loop in Ruby

```ruby
1.upto(10) { |x| puts x }
```

Ruby has an active developer community both online and in local developer groups. The Ruby language website, *http://www.ruby-lang.org*, has more information about these user groups. A wide array of books about Ruby have been published, perhaps most famously *Programming Ruby: The Pragmatic Programmers's Guide* (Pragmatic Bookshelf) by Dave Thomas, Chad Fowler, and Andy Hunt, known as the "pickaxe book" because of its cover, and *The Ruby Programming Language* by David Flanagan and Yukihiro Matsumoto (O'Reilly).

JRuby

JRuby began its life as a direct port of the C-based interpreter for Ruby 1.6 written by a programmer named Jan Arne Petersen in 2001. For the next few years, it was an interesting project, but had serious performance limitations. Following the release of Ruby 1.8 in 2003 and then the release of the Ruby on Rails web framework in 2004, a significant amount of effort has been put into developing JRuby, especially in the areas of compatibility and performance. In September 2006, Sun Microsystems effectively endorsed JRuby when it hired two of the lead developers, Charles Nutter and Thomas Enebo, to work on JRuby full-time. Since then, a third lead developer, Nick Sieger, has become a Sun employee.[†]

For Sun, JRuby represents an opportunity to expand the prevalence of the Java Virtual Machine. Although the JVM was originally tied very closely to the Java language, the emergence of projects like JRuby, Jython (a Java implementation of Python), Groovy (a scripting language inspired by Ruby), and Scala (a functional/object-oriented programming language) have proved that the JVM can host a wide variety of languages. This trend culminated with the development of Java Specification Request (JSR) 223, Scripting for the Java Platform. JSR 223 defines a standard API (Application Programming Interface) for scripting languages to integrate with the JVM. Implementations of the JSR 223 API are available for 25 different languages from *https://scripting.dev.java .net*. This API will be discussed further in Chapter 3.

For users, JRuby represents a different opportunity: to take advantage of the power of a dynamic language such as Ruby while still being able to leverage existing Java libraries and application servers. This area will be explored in the first two chapters.

With the release of JRuby 1.1 in April 2008, JRuby has closed the performance gap with the C Ruby interpreter and is in many cases faster. In terms of compatibility, the JRuby project strives to duplicate the behavior of the standard Ruby interpreter whenever possible, even at the expense of consistency with Java. Most of the core Ruby classes are included, as is much of the standard Ruby library, the RubyGems package management system, RDoc documentation support, and the Rake build system. Despite these efforts at compatibility, there are some areas where JRuby deviates from behavior exhibited by the C Ruby interpreter. The most visible example of this is how JRuby handles threads. In this case, however, JRuby is actually *ahead* of the standard Ruby interpreter in that Ruby 2.0 is expected to have a similar threading model to what JRuby already supports.

This chapter goes through the JRuby installation process, some core Java/Ruby integration information, and finally a variety of IDE integration options.

[†] A fourth lead developer, Ola Bini, works for the influential IT consulting company ThoughtWorks.

1.1 Installing JRuby

Problem

You want to install JRuby.

Solution

Download and extract the latest binary release from the JRuby website, *http://www .jruby.org*. Add the *bin* directory to the PATH environment variable.

Discussion

Windows

The JRuby website makes binary releases available in both ZIP and TGZ file formats. Since Windows XP, Windows operating system software has included support for extracting ZIP files. Commercial and open source software packages are available that include support for TGZ files, such as WinZip (*http://www.winzip.com*), 7-Zip (*http:// www.7-zip.org*), and IZArc (*http://www.izarc.com*).

It is not necessary to install JRuby in any particular location on your computer. My preference is to install Java libraries and executables in subdirectories of C:\java. The results of extracting the binary for the latest release at the time of this writing, 1.1, can be seen in Figure 1-1.

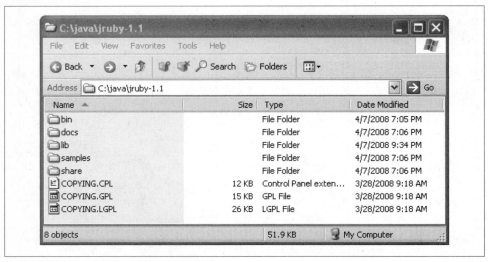

Figure 1-1. Extracted JRuby binary build

After extraction, JRuby is ready to be used. The simplest way to see JRuby in action is by running jirb, JRuby's version of Interactive Ruby (irb). Like irb, jirb allows you to execute Ruby statements and immediately see the results of each statement. JRuby includes both command-line and GUI versions of `jirb` in the *bin* directory. The command-line version, seen in Figure 1-2, can be run by executing *bin\jirb.bat*; the GUI version, seen in Figure 1-3, can be run by executing *bin\jirb_swing.bat*. In both figures, some trivial Ruby code has been executed. You can see that both the output of the `puts` method (`Hello World`) and its result (`nil`) have been output.

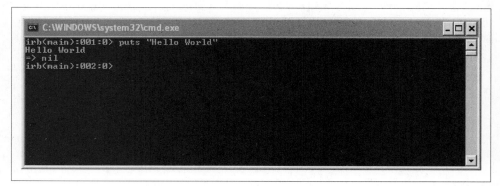

Figure 1-2. Command-line jirb

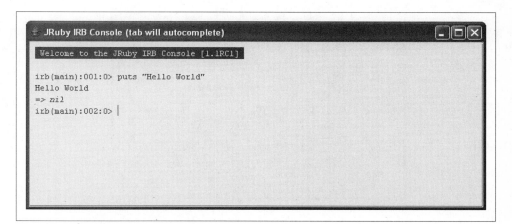

Figure 1-3. jirb GUI

 If you launch either *jirb.bat* or *jirb_swing.bat* from Windows Explorer and all you see is a black window appear and then disappear quickly, the likely cause is that you do not have the `JAVA_HOME` environment variable set, or the value of this environment variable is incorrect. To set environment variables in Windows, use the System control panel's Advanced tab. `JAVA_HOME` should point to the directory in which you have Java installed.

You can also test JRuby from the command line by using the -e (evaluate) option:

```
C:\java\jruby-1.1\bin\jruby -e "puts 'Hello World'"
```

To avoid having to retype the full path to JRuby's *bin* directory, add it to the PATH environment variable by opening the System control panel and clicking on the Advanced tab. On the Advanced tab, click the Environment Variables button. This will bring up the Environment Variables dialog, seen in Figure 1-4. Using the New and Edit buttons for System variables, add a JRUBY_HOME environment variable and also prepend the value %JRUBY_HOME%\bin to the PATH environment variable. You could also simply prepend the full path to the *bin* directory to PATH, but using a separate environment variable makes upgrading a bit easier.

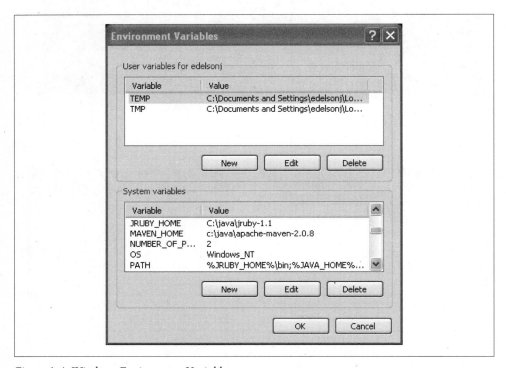

Figure 1-4. Windows Environment Variables

Once you have configured the environment variables, click OK. These changes will only be reflected in newly opened windows (something to keep in mind if you have any command-line windows open). After adding the *bin* directory to your PATH, you can then simply run the test shown previously by executing:

```
jruby -e "puts 'Hello World'"
```

Linux and Mac OS X

The JRuby website makes binary releases available in both ZIP and TGZ file formats. Although most Linux distributions and OS X include utilities for extracting both types of files, TGZ files are preferable because files extracted from them include permission settings, something that is not the case with ZIP files.

 The JPackage Project at *http://www.jpackage.org* has a release available in RPM format. At the time of this writing, JPackage did not have the latest JRuby version available, but that may not be the case when you're reading this.

If you have root privileges on the system where you want JRuby installed, you should install JRuby based on whatever standards already exist. This could mean installing JRuby in */usr/local/jruby*, */usr/share/jruby*, or */opt/jruby*, among other options. Based on OS X conventions, Mac users should install in */opt/local/jruby* or */usr/local/jruby*. If you do not have root privileges, then you likely need to install it inside your home directory, such as *~/jruby*. By default, the JRuby releases extract to a directory containing the version number, so we'll simply create a symbolic link between *~/jruby* and *~/jruby-1.1*. This will facilitate upgrades later:

```
$ cd ~
$ tar -xzf jruby-bin-1.1.tar.gz
$ ln -s jruby-1.1 jruby
```

Set `JRUBY_HOME` to the installation directory and add JRuby's *bin* directory to the `PATH` environment variable; add lines to the *~/.profile* similar to those in Example 1-4.

Example 1-4. Example .profile file that adds JRuby to the PATH environment variable

```
export JRUBY_HOME=~/jruby
export PATH=$JRUBY_HOME/bin:$PATH
```

Once the *bin* directory has been added to your `PATH`, you can test the install by running a simple Ruby script:

```
$ jruby -e "puts 'Hello World'"
Hello World
```

 You must add JRuby's *bin* directory to your `PATH` in order to use any of the command-line utilities included with JRuby, including `jirb`.

See Also

- Recipe 8.1, "Building JRuby from Source"
- Recipe 1.3, "Using Both Ruby and JRuby"

1.2 Managing Packages with RubyGems

Problem

You want to install Ruby on Rails or other Ruby packages for use with JRuby.

Solution

Use the RubyGems support built into JRuby. Once JRuby has been installed, you can immediately start using RubyGems to manage Ruby packages by running the *gem* script included in JRuby's *bin* directory. To install a package, run:

```
$ gem install packagename
```

For example, to install the Ruby on Rails web framework, use:

```
$ gem install rails
```

Discussion

RubyGems is the standard package management and distribution system for Ruby packages. There are thousands of packages, referred to as *gems*, available through the default RubyGems repository at *http://gems.rubyforge.org*. Although some gems are specific to the C Ruby implementation or JRuby, most are compatible with any Ruby implementation.

Common RubyGems commands include `install`, `query`, `update`, `uninstall`, and `rdoc`. The full list can be output by using the `help` command:

```
$ gem help commands
GEM commands are:

    build           Build a gem from a gemspec
    cert            Manage RubyGems certificates and signing settings
    check           Check installed gems
    cleanup         Clean up old versions of installed gems in the local
                    repository
    contents        Display the contents of the installed gems
    dependency      Show the dependencies of an installed gem
    environment     Display information about the RubyGems environment
    fetch           Download a gem and place it in the current directory
    generate_index  Generates the index files for a gem server directory
    help            Provide help on the 'gem' command
    install         Install a gem into the local repository
    list            Display all gems whose name starts with STRING
    lock            Generate a lockdown list of gems
    mirror          Mirror a gem repository
    outdated        Display all gems that need updates
    pristine        Restores installed gems to pristine condition from files
                    located in the gem cache
    query           Query gem information in local or remote repositories
    rdoc            Generates RDoc for pre-installed gems
    search          Display all gems whose name contains STRING
```

```
server          Documentation and gem repository HTTP server
sources         Manage the sources and cache file RubyGems uses to search
                for gems
specification   Display gem specification (in yaml)
uninstall       Uninstall gems from the local repository
unpack          Unpack an installed gem to the current directory
update          Update the named gems (or all installed gems) in the local
                repository
which           Find the location of a library

For help on a particular command, use 'gem help COMMAND'.

Commands may be abbreviated, so long as they are unambiguous.
e.g., 'gem i rake' is short for 'gem install rake'.
```

See Also

- The RubyGems Manuals, *http://rubygems.org*
- Recipe 1.3, "Using Both Ruby and JRuby"

1.3 Using Both Ruby and JRuby

Problem

You have Ruby and JRuby installed on the same computer and want to ensure that a Ruby script is processed by the correct interpreter.

Solution

Use the -S command-line argument for the *ruby* and *jruby* executables. For example, RubyGems is traditionally invoked with a command like:

```
gem install rails
```

Instead, use:

```
$ jruby -S gem install rails
```

or:

```
$ ruby -S gem install rails
```

Discussion

Popular Ruby packages such as Rake, Ruby on Rails, and RubyGems include their own executable Ruby scripts that most guides, both online and print, instruct you to invoke directly. Whether these scripts run with Ruby or JRuby depends on how you've configured the PATH environment variable, which platform you use, and what package is involved. Because there are so many variables, this recipe prescribes using a single, consistent method, passing the script name through the -S command-line argument to either the *ruby* or *jruby* executables.

The `-S` command-line option instructs Ruby and JRuby to load a script file from the PATH. JRuby includes its own copies of the Rake and RubyGems scripts in *bin/rake* and *bin/gem*, respectively, but they are verbatim copies of the original scripts. As a result, it doesn't matter which version of the script you execute, *only the interpreter with which you execute it.*

This advice is particularly significant in the context of the RubyGems script, *gem*. To create a new Rails application, you could run either:

```
$ ruby -S rails sampleapp
```

or:

```
$ jruby -S rails sampleapp
```

and see the same result. However, running:

```
$ ruby -S gem install rails
```

and:

```
$ jruby -S gem install rails
```

will install the Rails gem in two different locations. You can see this by passing environment to the *gem* script:

```
$ ruby -S gem environment
RubyGems Environment:
  - RUBYGEMS VERSION: 1.0.1 (1.0.1)
  - RUBY VERSION: 1.8.5 (2007-09-24 patchlevel 114) [i386-linux]
  - INSTALLATION DIRECTORY: /usr/lib/ruby/gems/1.8
  - RUBY EXECUTABLE: /usr/bin/ruby
  - RUBYGEMS PLATFORMS:
    - ruby
    - x86-linux
  - GEM PATHS:
    - /usr/lib/ruby/gems/1.8
  - GEM CONFIGURATION:
    - :update_sources => true
    - :verbose => true
    - :benchmark => false
    - :backtrace => false
    - :bulk_threshold => 1000
  - REMOTE SOURCES:
    - http://gems.rubyforge.org
$ jruby -S gem environment
RubyGems Environment:
  - RUBYGEMS VERSION: 1.0.1 (1.0.1)
  - RUBY VERSION: 1.8.6 (2008-01-07 patchlevel 5512) [java]
  - INSTALLATION DIRECTORY: /home/justin/jruby-1.1/lib/ruby/gems/1.8
  - RUBY EXECUTABLE: /home/justin/jruby-1.1/bin/jruby
  - RUBYGEMS PLATFORMS:
    - ruby
    - universal-java-1.6
  - GEM PATHS:
    - /home/justin/jruby-1.1/lib/ruby/gems/1.8
```

```
      - GEM CONFIGURATION:
        - :update_sources => true
        - :verbose => true
        - :benchmark => false
        - :backtrace => false
        - :bulk_threshold => 1000
      - REMOTE SOURCES:
        - http://gems.rubyforge.org
```

See Also

- Recipe 1.2, "Managing Packages with RubyGems"

1.4 Sharing RubyGems

Problem

You already have a number of RubyGems installed and want to use those gems from JRuby without reinstalling the gems.

Solution

Set the GEM_HOME environment variable to your existing RubyGems installation location. This value can be seen in the output of gem environment, where it is referred to as the installation directory:

```
$ ruby -S gem environment | grep -i 'installation directory'
- INSTALLATION DIRECTORY: /usr/lib/ruby/gems/1.8
$ export GEM_HOME=/usr/lib/ruby/gems/1.8
$ jruby -S gem environment | grep -i 'installation directory'
- INSTALLATION DIRECTORY: /usr/lib/ruby/gems/1.8
```

Discussion

Whereas some RubyGems are implemented entirely in Ruby, many are implemented in a combination of Ruby and C (or, in a growing number of cases, Ruby and Java). Pure-Ruby gems can be installed using either JRuby or C Ruby. However, those implemented in a mixture can only be installed using a compatible interpreter. The list of supported platforms for each interpreter can be seen in the output of gem environment. Because the RubyGems runtime knows this list of supported platforms, it is possible to mix gems supporting different platforms in the same directory; the runtime will select the appropriate libraries.

1.5 Referencing Java Classes from Ruby

Problem

You want to write Ruby code that uses one or more Java classes.

Solution

First, you need to tell JRuby that you will be referencing Java classes from your Ruby code. Do this by including an `include` declaration at the top of your Ruby file:

```
include Java
```

The syntax for referencing a specific Java class depends on the package in which the class resides. For packages starting with `java`, `javax`, `org`, and `com`, you can simply reference the fully qualified class name or use an `import` statement, as shown in Example 1-5.

Example 1-5. Creating a Java TreeMap from Ruby

```
# using the fully-qualified class name
map = java.util.TreeMap.new

# using an import statement
import java.util.TreeMap
map = TreeMap.new
```

For classes that reside in a package that does not begin with `java`, `javax`, `org`, or `com`, as well as classes in the default package, you need to use the `include_class` function, as in Example 1-6.

Example 1-6. Referencing a Java class with include_class

```
include_class 'EDU.oswego.cs.dl.util.concurrent.ConcurrentHashMap'

map = ConcurrentHashMap.new
```

 The `include_class` function can also handle classes in packages starting with `java`, `javax`, `org`, and `com` if you don't want to switch back and forth.

The `include_class` function can also be used to create aliases in cases where a Java class name conflicts with a Ruby class name. To do this, pass a block to the function. Example 1-7 aliases the Java `String` class as `JString` so that it does not conflict with Ruby's `String` class.

Example 1-7. Creating an alias to avoid class name conflicts

```
include Java

include_class 'java.lang.String' do |package,name|
    "JString"
end

p JString.new("A quick brown fox").indexOf("brown")
```

You can pass multiple class names to the `include_class` as a list. In this case, you could provide the appropriate alias using a `case` statement, as seen in Example 1-8.

Example 1-8. Aliasing multiple classes with case

```
include_class ['java.lang.String','java.lang.Integer'] do |package,name|
    case name
    when "String"
        "JString"
    when "Integer"
        "JInteger"
    end
end
```

An alternative to this aliasing technique is wrapping a Java package in a Ruby module using the `include_package` function, as seen in Example 1-9.

Example 1-9. Wrapping a Java package with a Ruby module

```
include Java

module JavaLang
    include_package 'java.lang'
end

p JavaLang::String.new("A quick brown fox").indexOf("brown")
```

Discussion

JRuby makes referencing Java classes relatively natural from the perspective of a Java developer. For the most commonly used packages, you can use `import` just as you would in Java code.

When calling methods on a Java class, JRuby handles some type conversion for you—instances of basic Ruby classes such as `FixNum`, `Float`, and `String` are converted to instances of the corresponding Java classes when passed to Java objects. JRuby includes implementations of the `java.util.List` and `java.util.Map` interfaces for handling Ruby `Array` and `Hash` objects. Ruby `Array` objects can also be coerced into Java `Array` objects by calling the `to_java` method. Example 1-10 includes a combination of Java and Ruby code, which demonstrates this functionality.

Example 1-10. Ruby to Java type conversion

```java
package org.jrubycookbook.ch01;

import java.io.PrintWriter;
import java.io.StringWriter;
import java.util.Arrays;
import java.util.Collections;
import java.util.List;

import org.jruby.Ruby;
import org.jruby.javasupport.JavaEmbedUtils;

public class PrintJavaClass {

    // Output the class and interface list for a single object
    public String output(Object o) {
        String className = o.getClass().getName();
        List<Class> interfaces = Arrays.asList(o.getClass().getInterfaces());

        return String.format("%s, implements %s\n", className, interfaces);
    }

    // Output the class and interface list for each object in an array
    public String output(Object[] objects) {
        PrintWriter writer = new PrintWriter(new StringWriter());
        for (Object o : objects) {
            String className = o.getClass().getName();
            List<Class> interfaces = Arrays
                    .asList(o.getClass().getInterfaces());

            writer.printf("%s (inside array), implements %s\n", className,
                    interfaces);
        }
        return writer.toString();
    }

    public static void main(String[] args) {
        Ruby runtime = JavaEmbedUtils.initialize(Collections.EMPTY_LIST);
        String script = "@printer = org.jrubycookbook.ch01.PrintJavaClass.new\n"
                + "def output(o)\n"
                + "puts \"#{o.to_s} - #{@printer.output(o)}\"\n"
                + "end\n"
                + "output(1)\n"
                + "output(0.5)\n"
                + "output('string')\n"
                + "output(true)\n"
                + "output([4, 8, 15, 16, 23, 42])\n"
                + "output([4, 8, 15, 16, 23, 42].to_java)\n"
                + "output({ 'NY' => 'New York', 'MA' => 'Massachusetts'})\n";

        runtime.evalScriptlet(script);
        JavaEmbedUtils.terminate(runtime);
    }
}
```

See Recipe 3.1 for an explanation of the `JavaEmbedUtils` class used in Example 1-10.

When executed, this class outputs:

```
1 - Class is java.lang.Long, implements [interface java.lang.Comparable]
0.5 - Class is java.lang.Double, implements [interface java.lang.Comparable]
string - Class is java.lang.String, implements [interface java.io.Serializable,\
  interface java.lang.Comparable, interface java.lang.CharSequence]
true - Class is java.lang.Boolean, implements [interface java.io.Serializable,\
  interface java.lang.Comparable]
4815162342 - Class is org.jruby.RubyArray, implements [interface java.util.List]
[Ljava.lang.Object;@8b058b - Received an array
In array: class is java.lang.Integer, implements [interface java.lang.Comparable]
In array: class is java.lang.Integer, implements [interface java.lang.Comparable]
In array: class is java.lang.Integer, implements [interface java.lang.Comparable]
In array: class is java.lang.Integer, implements [interface java.lang.Comparable]
In array: class is java.lang.Integer, implements [interface java.lang.Comparable]
In array: class is java.lang.Integer, implements [interface java.lang.Comparable]
NYNew YorkMAMassachusetts - Class is org.jruby.RubyHash, implements\
  [interface java.util.Map]
```

JRuby provides access to public static methods and variables through the `::` operator. Example 1-11 shows how you would access the static methods and variables of the Java `Math` class.

Example 1-11. Accessing static methods and variables

```
require 'java'

puts java.lang.Math::max(100,200)
puts java.lang.Math::PI
```

1.6 Converting a Ruby Array into a Java Array

Problem

You need to pass a Ruby array to a method that accepts a Java array of a specific type.

Solution

Call the Ruby array's `to_java` method with an argument specifying the component type of the array. For example, creating an array of `javax.xml.transform.stream.Stream Source` objects would be done like this:

```
import javax.xml.transform.stream.StreamSource

cnn = StreamSource.new "http://rss.cnn.com/rss/cnn_topstories.rss"
mtv = StreamSource.new "http://www.mtv.com/rss/news/news_full.jhtml"
```

```
# Call a transforming Java API. This method would have been declared
# with this signature:
# public String transform(StreamSource[] sources)
p transformer.transform([cnn,mtv].to_java(StreamSource))
```

Primitives, as well as `java.lang.String`, have Ruby symbols assigned to them. For example, to create an array of `int` primitives:

```
[1,2,3,4,5,6,7,8,9,10].to_java(:int)
```

Discussion

This JRuby feature is critical for accessing Java APIs. For example, calling a method through Java Management Extensions (JMX) involves passing two arrays to the `invoke()` method of `javax.management.MBeanServer`, one of `Object` instances, storing the method parameters, and one of `String` instances, storing the method signature. To call `invoke()` from JRuby, you would do something like this:

```
brokerName = ObjectName.new('org.apache.activemq:BrokerName=localhost,Type=Broker')
params = ["MyQueue"].to_java()
signature = ["java.lang.String"].to_java(:string)
server.invoke(brokerName, 'addQueue', params, signature)
```

1.7 Adding JAR Files to the Classpath

Problem

You want to reference a Java class which is contained in a JAR file that isn't already included in your classpath.

Solution

Call Ruby's `require` method with the path to the JAR file. This path can be relative to the current working directory:

```
require 'lib/commons-logging-1.1.jar'
```

or an absolute path:

```
require '/opt/java/commons-logging/bin/commons-logging-1.1.jar'
```

If you are using Windows, this path can have either type of slash:

```
require 'c:\java\commons-logging-1.1\bin\commons-logging-1.1.jar'
# or
require 'c:/java/commons-logging-1.1/bin/commons-logging-1.1.jar'
```

Discussion

Although this is an extremely useful feature of JRuby, it should be used with caution, especially if you use absolute paths that are platform- and installation-specific. Relative paths can seem like a better solution, but are actually more limiting, as they are evaluated from the current working directory, not the script's directory. Yet all is not lost.

An interesting aspect of this feature of JRuby is that the JAR file is added to the classpath dynamically, while the application is running. This allows you to use Ruby's string interpolation functionality to create absolute paths. Example 1-12 includes a method that creates a path to a JAR file in a local Maven repository.‡

Example 1-12. Creating a JAR file path dynamically

```
# Set the HOME environment variable if USERPROFILE is set
ENV['HOME'] = ENV['USERPROFILE'] if (ENV['USERPROFILE'])

def require_from_maven(group,artifact,version)
    maven_path = "#{group}/#{artifact}/#{version}/#{artifact}-#{version}.jar"
    require "#{ENV['HOME']}/.m2/repository/#{maven_path}"
end
```

Application code could use `require` to include this script and then use the `require_from_maven` method to reference a specific JAR file:

```
require 'require_from_maven'
require_from_maven "commons-logging", "commons-logging", "1.1"
```

1.8 Extending a Java Class in Ruby

Problem

To use a Java API, you need to create a Ruby class that subclasses a Java class.

Solution

Use the standard Ruby superclassing operator `<` and specify the Java class you want to subclass. Example 1-13 shows a Ruby class that extends the Java `Thread` class and overrides the `run()` method.

Example 1-13. Subclassing a Java class in Ruby

```
include Java

class MyThread < java.lang.Thread
    def run
        puts 'hello world'
    end
end

MyThread.new.start
```

---

‡ This use of the Maven repository is naïve, as it assumes the JAR file is already in the local repository. Buildr, a build system for Java written in Ruby, includes support for downloading JAR files from remote Maven repositories. More information about Buildr can be found in Chapter 6.

Discussion

The fact that the same syntax is used to extend both Java and Ruby classes is an important design feature of JRuby, as it furthers the seamless integration between the two languages.

 One notable exception to this recipe is classes that use Java 5 generics. Currently, these cannot be subclassed with Ruby classes.

Abstract Java classes can also be extended by Ruby classes. Examples 1-14 and 1-15 show an example of an abstract Java class and a concrete Ruby class that extends the former. The `hello()` method, declared abstract in the Java class, is implemented in the Ruby class.

Example 1-14. An abstract Java class

```java
package org.jrubycookbook.ch01;

public abstract class AbstractElement {
    public abstract void hello();

    public void sayHello(int count) {
        for (int i = 0; i < count; i++) {
            hello();
        }
    }
}
```

Example 1-15. Ruby class that subclasses an abstract Java class

```ruby
include Java

import org.jrubycookbook.ch01.AbstractElement

class RubyElement < AbstractElement
    def hello
        puts 'hello world'
    end
end

RubyElement.new.sayHello 5
```

1.9 Implementing a Java Interface in Ruby

Problem

To use a Java API, you need to create a Ruby class that implements a Java interface.

Solution

Create your class with method names that match the names in the Java interface. As of version 1.1, JRuby runtime supports the use of *duck typing* for implementing Java interfaces. Duck typing, seen in many dynamic languages, including Ruby, means that the type of an object is determined based on the methods implemented by the object. Example 1-16 shows this technique in action as a new Java thread by passing the constructor an object that implements the `java.lang.Runnable` interface. The `HelloThread` class contains a zero-argument `run` method that corresponds to the method defined in `java.lang.Runnable`. JRuby requires no additional type information in the `HelloThread` class to instantiate the `Thread` object.

Example 1-16. Ruby implementation of a Java interface

```
include Java

class HelloThread
    def run
        puts 'hello world'
    end
end

java.lang.Thread.new(HelloThread.new).start
```

Discussion

There are few situations when duck typing isn't sufficient and you'll need to provide additional type information to the interpreter. One case is when a duck-typed JRuby object is passed as an argument to an overloaded Java method. Without additional Java type information, the JRuby interpreter doesn't definitively know which method to execute. The solution is to use Ruby's `include` statement to assign an explicit Java interface to a Ruby class. This provides the JRuby interpreter with enough information about the object to execute the correct method. In Example 1-17, the `HelloThread` class is assigned the `Runnable` interface. As a result, JRuby calls the desired `exec()` method and `runnable` is output to the console.

Example 1-17. Declaring Java interfaces in JRuby

Balloon.java

```
public interface Balloon {
    void pop();
}
```

Bubble.java

```
public interface Bubble {
    void pop();
}
```

Child.java

```java
public class Child{
    public void give(Bubble bubble){
        System.out.println("Thanks for the bubble.");
        bubble.pop();
    }
    public void give(Balloon balloon){
        System.out.println("Thanks for the balloon.");
        balloon.pop();
    }
}
```

main.rb

```ruby
include Java

class MylarBalloon
    include Java::Balloon
    def pop
      puts 'Oh No!!!'
    end
end

child = Java::Child.new
child.give(MylarBalloon.new)
```

Because Ruby scripts implicitly create a top-level class, it is not even necessary to define a new class to implement a Java interface. This functionality, seen in Example 1-18, can be especially useful when prototyping and testing.

Example 1-18. JRuby working with Java interfaces—condensed version

```ruby
include Java

def pop
    puts 'Bang'
end

child = Java::Child.new
child.give(self)
```

Ruby modules are a natural fit to help implement Java interfaces. In some ways they resemble abstract Java classes, but Ruby modules are different in that a class may include many modules. Example 1-19 shows the use of a module to implement a Java interface and the reuse of this module.

Example 1-19. Implementing a Java interface with a module

```ruby
include Java

module RunModule
    def run
        1.upto(10) { |i| puts "You're number #{i}" }
    end
```

```
end

class HelloThread
    include RunModule
end

java.lang.Thread.new(HelloThread.new).start
```

JRuby allows you to create an instance of the interface by using the `impl` method that's dynamically attached to all Java interfaces. The method accepts a block as an argument that is executed for every function call in the interface. The block defines two arguments: the name of the method in the interface that initiated the block's execution, and a variable input parameter to accommodate the method arguments. Example 1-20 uses the `impl` method to define the sorting behavior for a Java `Comparator`.

Example 1-20. Using JRuby's impl method

```
include Java

v = java.util.Vector.new
v.add_element("Lions")
v.add_element("Tigers")
v.add_element("Bears")

java.util.Collections::sort(v, java.util.Comparator.impl do |method, *args|
  case method.to_s
    when "compare"
      args[0] <=> args[1]
    when "equals"
      args[0] == args[1]
  end
end)

v.each do |val|
  puts val
end
```

Another interesting technique of working with an interface is to use a Ruby block as the input to a method where you would normally use a single-method Java interface. The Ruby block style can be used with nonoverloaded methods that expect to be called with a single argument that is a Java interface. When a block is passed to such a method, the JRuby runtime attempts to generate a proxy object that implements the interface. Overloaded and multiple methods make this process ambiguous and unworkable. Example 1-21 illustrates how this feature can make the Java Swing development significantly more concise.

Example 1-21. Implementing a Java interface with a Ruby block

```
frame = javax.swing.JFrame.new
frame.set_size 500,200

a = javax.swing.JButton.new("hello")
```

```
b = javax.swing.JButton.new("world")

#define the function using a block
a.add_action_listener do |evt|
  puts 'hello'
end

# define the function using a Ruby Proc
p = lambda{ |evt| puts 'world'}
b.add_action_listener &p

frame.add a
frame.add b
frame.set_layout(java.awt.GridLayout.new(1, 2))
frame.show
```

A Ruby `Proc` object can also be passed once it is transformed into a Ruby block using the `&` operator.

 Java interfaces that define a single method are sometimes referred to as *single abstract method types*, abbreviated as *SAM types*. All of the proposals for adding closures/blocks to Java 7 attempt to make implementation of these types significantly simpler and closer to what JRuby provides.

See Also

- Recipe 5.1, "Creating Swing Applications"

1.10 Opening Java Classes with JRuby

Problem

You want to add methods to a Java class.

Solution

Import the Java class so that the class can be referenced, and add methods as you would to any Ruby class.

Discussion

In Ruby, class definitions are never finalized; new methods can be added at any time. This is perhaps one of the most significant differences between Java and Ruby. In Java, class definitions are tightly bound to filenames and directory structures. The complete definition of the Java class `java.util.HashMap` will be found in a file named */java/util/ HashMap.class*. In Ruby, no such relationship exists and classes can be defined across multiple source files. With JRuby, it's possible to apply this language feature to Java classes. Example 1-22 shows a simple example of enhancing the `java.util.HashMap` class with a method named `is?`.

Example 1-22. Adding a method to HashMap

```
include Java

import java.util.HashMap

class HashMap
    def is?(key,value)
        value == get(key)
    end
end
```

As you can see in this example, within the new method we can call methods defined by the original Java class. Once this code is executed, JRuby instances of the `HashMap` class, *including those already created*, will have this new method. This even applies to instances of the class created by Java code. Examples 1-23 and 1-24 contain a Java class that creates a `HashMap` object and Ruby code that opens the `HashMap` class and exercises the new method.

Example 1-23. A simple class to generate a HashMap object

```
package org.jrubycookbook.ch01;

import java.util.*;

public class MapMaker {
    public static Map makeMap() {
        Map m = new HashMap();
        m.put("k1", "v1");
        m.put("k2", "v2");
        return m;
    }
}
```

Example 1-24. Applying open class semantics to an instance created with Java code

```
include Java

import java.util.HashMap
import org.jrubycookbook.ch01.MapMaker

h = MapMaker.makeMap()

class HashMap
    def isNot?(key,value)
        value != get(key)
    end
end
```

```
puts (h.isNot? 'k1', 'v1')
puts (h.isNot? 'k2', 'v3')
```

However, any added methods are only visible to the JRuby runtime. If you were to pass an instance of this modified `HashMap` class to Java code, the new methods would not be available.

JRuby also includes a utility method called `extend_proxy` that allows you to add new methods to all implementations of a particular interface. Example 1-24 could be rewritten to use this functionality so as to work with any implementation of `java.util.Map`. This can be seen in Example 1-25.

Example 1-25. Using extend_proxy to open all implementations of an interface

```
include Java

import org.jrubycookbook.ch01.MapMaker

h = MapMaker.makeMap()

JavaUtilities.extend_proxy('java.util.Map') do
    def isNot?(key,value)
        value != get(key)
    end
end

puts (h.isNot? 'k1', 'v1')
puts (h.isNot? 'k2', 'v3')
```

See Also

- Recipe 1.5, "Referencing Java Classes from Ruby"

1.11 Setting Up Eclipse for JRuby Development

Problem

You use the Eclipse Integrated Development Environment (IDE) for Ruby development and want to run Ruby code easily with the JRuby interpreter.

Solution

When using the Ruby Development Tools (RDT) plugin, create a new Ruby VM definition that is pointed at your JRuby installation location and whose type is set to JRuby VM. When using the Dynamic Language Toolkit (DLTK) plugin, create a new Ruby interpreter definition that references the JRuby launch script: *bin\jruby.bat* (for Windows) or *bin/jruby* (for Linux and Mac OS X) from your JRuby installation.

Discussion

Both RDT and DLTK can be configured to work with multiple Ruby interpreters. RDT has a specific setting available for the JRuby interpreter, whereas DLTK simply treats JRuby as a generic Ruby interpreter.

RDT

RDT, available from *http://rubyeclipse.sourceforge.net*, supports configuration of Ruby interpreters based on the installation directory. To add JRuby as an interpreter, open the Preferences dialog and locate the Installed Interpreters page. Click the Add button to open the Add RubyVM dialog (seen in Figure 1-5). In this dialog, select JRuby VM as the RubyVM type and select the JRuby installation directory as the RubyVM home directory. You can also override the display name with something more user-friendly. Once you're satisfied with the settings, click OK.

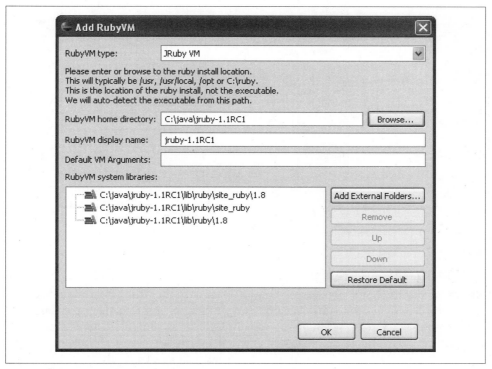

Figure 1-5. RDT Add RubyVM dialog

DLTK

The Dynamic Language Toolkit project, hosted at *http://www.eclipse.org/dltk*, is a broad project sponsored by the Eclipse Foundation to provide general support for dynamic languages in the Eclipse development environment. Currently, support is available through the DLKT project for Ruby, TCL, and Python. The DLTK Ruby plugin does not make a distinction between a standard Ruby interpreter and the JRuby interpreter. Just as when configuring RDT, open the Preferences dialog and locate the Interpreters page. Click the Add button to open the "Add interpreter" dialog, seen in Figure 1-6. Select the *bin\jruby.bat* (for Windows) or *bin/jruby* (for Linux and Mac OS X) as the interpreter executable. As with RDT, you can change the interpreter name to something more user-friendly. Finally, click OK to add the interpreter.

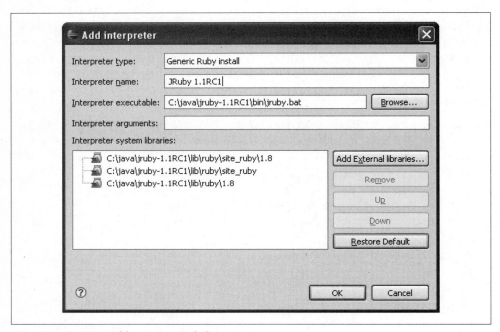

Figure 1-6. DLTK "Add interpreter" dialog

Running JRuby as a Java application

Although both RDT and DLTK can easily interface with the JRuby interpreter because they are both designed for Ruby development, you are not able to manage the classpath used by the Java Virtual Machine inside which JRuby is running. This is a problem when referencing Java classes located in external JAR files. Since the JRuby interpreter is simply a Java class, it can be run as such within Eclipse. To do this, open the Run dialog by selecting "Open Run Dialog..." from the Run menu. Select Java Application and click the New button to create a new launch configuration. For the Main class, enter `org.jruby.Main`. In the Arguments tab, put the path to the Ruby file you want to run in the Program arguments section (along with any other application-specific arguments). The VM arguments should include the `jruby.base`, `jruby.home`, and `jruby.lib` system properties. Set `jruby.base` and `jruby.home` to the JRuby installation directory and `jruby.lib` to the JRuby *lib* directory for the last one. Eclipse has an expression language available to this dialog that allows you to reference the `JRUBY_HOME` environment variable while setting these properties with this value:

```
-Djruby.base="${env_var:JRUBY_HOME}" -Djruby.home="${env_var:JRUBY_HOME}"
-Djruby.lib="${env_var:JRUBY_HOME}/lib"
```

Finally, in the Classpath tab, add *bsf.jar* and *jruby.jar* from JRuby's *lib* directory and any other JAR files needed by your code. Then, click the Run button to execute.

Eclipse also supports expressions that prompt the user for input. You can use this functionality to make the launch configuration more reusable. You can prompt for a file, which opens the operating system's standard file selection dialog, with:

```
${file_prompt:Ruby Script Name}
```

To prompt specifically for a file within the workspace, use:

```
${resource_loc:${string_prompt:Ruby Script Name}}
```

In this case, the user is prompted for a location within the Eclipse workspace that is then converted into a filesystem path. You can see these expressions in use in Figure 1-7.

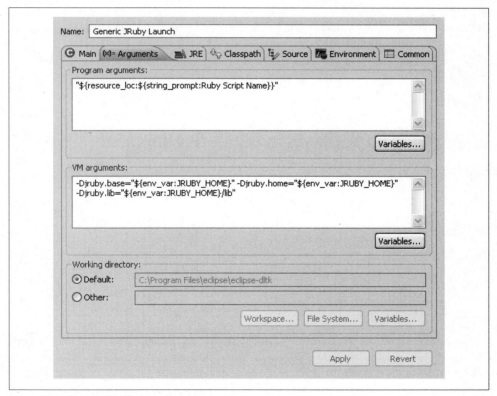

Figure 1-7. Generic JRuby launch configuration

Running this configuration opens a dialog, seen in Figure 1-8, where you can enter the workspace path to the Ruby script you want to execute. On subsequent executions, Eclipse automatically populates this dialog with the last value entered.

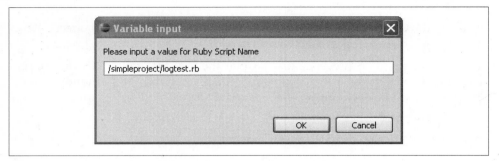

Figure 1-8. Eclipse variable input dialog

Note that using this type of launch configuration doesn't require using RDT or DLTK, although those plugins would still provide useful functionality, including code completion and RDoc integration.

See Also

- Recipe 1.1, "Installing JRuby"

1.12 Setting Up NetBeans for JRuby Development

Problem

You want to develop Ruby applications with NetBeans.

Solution

Download NetBeans 6.5 from *http://www.netbeans.org* and run the installer. NetBeans is available in a variety of bundles; both the Ruby and All bundles include support for Ruby development. In addition to Ruby, the All bundle includes support for Java, Web, Mobile, and C/C++, as well as both Apache Tomcat and Sun GlassFish application servers.

If you are already using NetBeans 6.5, Ruby support can be installed using the Plugins dialog, seen in Figure 1-9. This plugin adds new NetBeans project types for Ruby and Rails, graphical debuggers for Ruby and Rails, a Ruby Code Editor, and a RubyGems client.

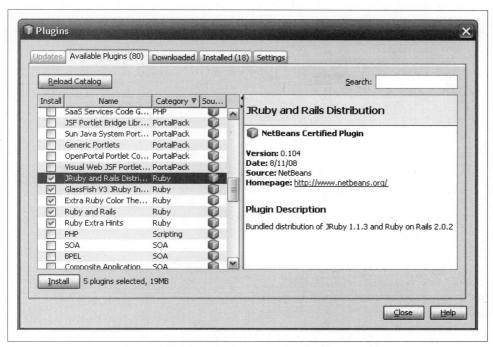

Figure 1-9. Installing the NetBeans Ruby plugin with the Plugins dialog

Once the Ruby plugin has been installed, use the Ruby page in the Ruby Platforms dialog seen in Figure 1-10 to manage the Ruby runtimes used by your projects. Notice the options to add new runtimes or modify an interpreter's gem repository location and debug level. By default, your Ruby project will use the JRuby runtime shipped with the Plugin, but you can assign a specific Ruby Platform to your application by using the project's properties dialog.

Discussion

After several years of playing second fiddle to Eclipse, Sun has recently made some significant investments in the NetBeans project, and it shows—nowhere more so than in the Ruby plugin. The NetBeans Ruby Code Editor includes syntax highlighting, code coloring, refactoring support, and powerful code completion capabilities. The code completion functionality can be seen in Figure 1-11. The editor displays a list of possible methods in a small window, including built-in and user-defined Ruby classes. Hitting the space bar at this point inserts the complete name into the editor.

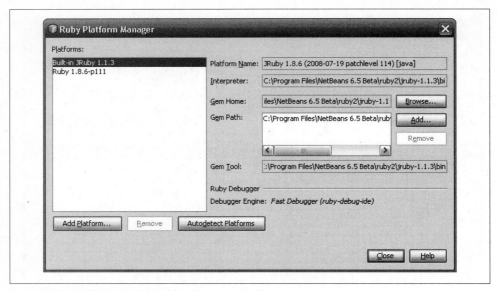

Figure 1-10. NetBeans Ruby Platform Manager dialog

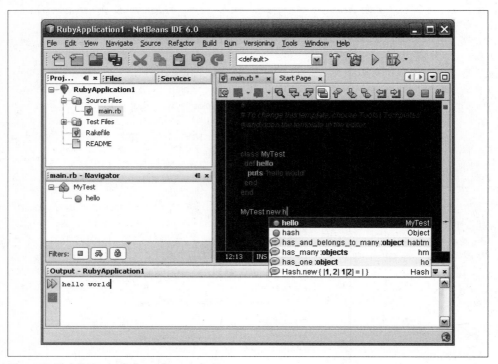

Figure 1-11. NetBeans Ruby code completion

You can also change the editor's font and highlighting colors or change the key bindings to match your personal preferences. Configuration is done in the Options dialog seen in Figure 1-12. Choose the Fonts & Colors tab and select a Profile from the list. OS X Ruby developers might be interested in a TextMate theme, Aloha (*http://pages.huikau .com/AlohaTheme.nbm*), for a more familiar color palette and highlighting rules. The Keymap page has bindings for Eclipse, Emacs, and older versions of NetBeans.

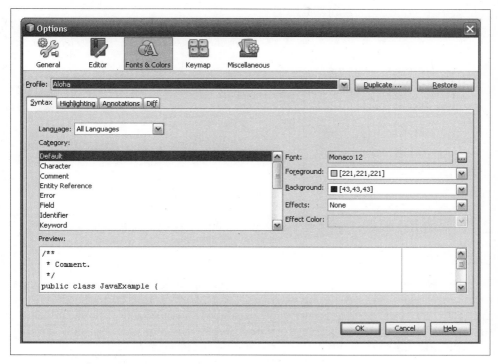

Figure 1-12. NetBeans Fonts & Colors Options dialog

See Also

- Recipe 2.11, "Deploying Rails on the GlassFish v2 Server"

1.13 Platform Detection in a JRuby Application

Problem

You would like to detect the platform used by the Ruby runtime and customize your code for a JRuby runtime environment.

Solution

You can detect whether your application is running in JRuby by evaluating the JRUBY_VERSION system variable. This value will always be defined in a JRuby application but never in any other Ruby runtime. The generate_random_number method in Example 1-26 uses the random number generator from the Java Math class in a JRuby environment; otherwise, the application calls Ruby's rand method.

Example 1-26. JRuby platform detection

```
class DetectionExample

  def generate_random_number
    if(defined?(JRUBY_VERSION))
     require 'java'
     puts 'executing java method'
     java.lang.Math.random
    else
     puts 'executing ruby method'
     rand(0)
    end
  end

end

d = DetectionExample.new
puts d.generate_random_number
```

Discussion

The RUBY_PLATFORM variable has information about the runtime environment and is set to java in JRuby. It was used with early versions of JRuby for platform detection, but the JRUBY_VERSION variable was later added to identify unequivocally that the code was running in JRuby and not another Ruby interpreter written in Java. The new variable also opened up the possibility for JRuby version-specific code.

## CHAPTER 2

JRuby on Rails

2.0 Introduction

Since its introduction in mid-2004, the Ruby on Rails web framework has rapidly gained a significant following within the web development community. It is the single largest factor in the overall increase in interest in the Ruby programming language. Likewise, JRuby's ability to run Rails applications inside a Java Virtual Machine has been a driver for interest in JRuby. This chapter explores some techniques for running Rails applications in a Java environment.

Ruby on Rails is a framework for developing web applications that follows the model-view-controller (MVC) architecture. The notion of Convention over Configuration is stressed throughout the framework, most prevalently within ActiveRecord, the object-relational-mapping (ORM) subsystem. ActiveRecord uses database metadata (table and column names) to dynamically define domain classes. Using ActiveRecord, simply adding a new column to a database table automatically adds a corresponding field to the related domain class.

Running Rails applications on JRuby provides several advantages:

- Rails applications can be deployed into existing Java EE containers such as Tomcat, JBoss, and GlassFish.

- Through Java Database Connectivity (JDBC), Rails applications can be connected to virtually any database for which a JDBC driver exists.

- Rails applications can access container-managed database connection pools through Java Naming and Directory Interface (JNDI).

In short, the combination of JRuby and Rails produces an enterprise-friendly package that blends seamlessly into an existing Java EE environment. From an application deployer's perspective, the Rails application is just another Java EE web application; if JNDI data sources are used, the application deployer never even needs to look at Rails configuration files.

Beyond JRuby, the primary library that provides the bridge between the Java EE container and Rails is called JRuby-Rack. JRuby-Rack is basically a Java servlet filter that dispatches requests to a Rails application running inside JRuby. JRuby-Rack creates a pool of JRuby runtime instances. Configuration of the JRuby-Rack servlet is discussed in Recipe 2.4. Early approaches to Java EE packaging and servlet integration used the GoldSpike project, but that code has been deprecated and replaced by JRuby-Rack.

In addition to JRuby-Rack, the JRuby team has produced Warbler, a tool for packaging a Rails application as a WAR file to facilitate deployment.

The middle part of this chapter goes through the specific steps required to deploy Rails applications onto major open source Java EE application servers. Although these recipes are very similar to one another, we thought it was important to provide the container-specific details. The last few recipes describe some additional configuration and usage scenarios when using JRuby and Rails together.

 As this book was going into production, the Rails team announced that the upcoming Rails 2.2 release would incorporate a number of changes designed to improve the thread-safety of the Rails core. Although it is too soon to tell how effective these changes will be, the likely outcome is that deploying Rails applications on JRuby will become substantially simpler. The JRuby team is closely tracking these developments and will undoubtedly continue to iterate the tools described in this chapter to take advantage of any new capabilities that are part of future Rails versions.

2.1 Installing and Setting Up Rails

Problem

You want to run Ruby on Rails with JRuby.

Solution

Install the latest Ruby on Rails gem with this command:

```
$ jruby -S gem install rails
```

If you're running Rails 2.x, it is recommended you install the **jruby-openssl** gem to take advantage of all the security features and session storage options. This gem is the Java implementation of the **openssl** gem:

```
$ jruby -S gem install jruby-openssl
```

Now create your Rails application with JRuby:

```
$ jruby -S rails MyKillerApplication
```

Test your new Rails application:

```
$ cd MyKillerApplication
$ jruby ./script/server
```

Open your browser and go to *http://localhost:3000*. You should see the ubiquitous Rails welcome screen, shown in Figure 2-1.

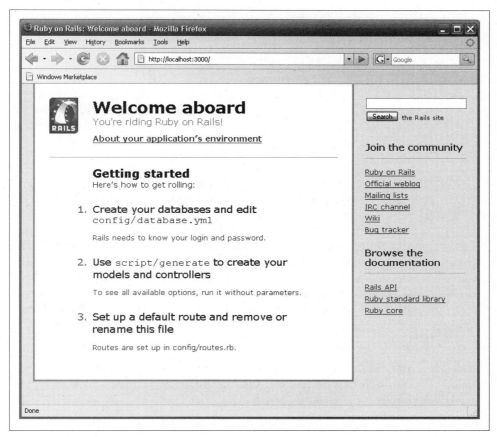

Figure 2-1. Ruby on Rails welcome screen

Discussion

The next step is to configure Rails to connect to your database. The JRuby team has made this easy by allowing Rails to use the familiar and widely supported Java JDBC drivers. You first need to install the `activerecord-jdbc-adapter` gem:

```
$ jruby -S gem install activerecord-jdbc-adapter -y --no-ri --no-rdoc
```

The gem allows the Rails database management system, ActiveRecord, to use a JDBC connection or connection pool for database access. This can be conveniently configured in the standard Rails *database.yml* file by specifying the JDBC URL or a JNDI address. The example *database.yml* in Example 2-1 is configured to use a JDBC connection in the development environment and container-provided `javax.sql.DataSource` with the

JNDI name `java:comp/env/jdbc/rails_db` in the production environment. Remember to include the JDBC driver in your classpath when using the standard `jdbc` adapter.

Example 2-1. Example database.yml using JDBC

```
development:
  adapter: jdbc
  url: jdbc:mysql://localhost:3306/jrubycookbook_development
  driver: com.mysql.jdbc.Driver
  username: jruby
  password: cookbook

production:
  adapter: jdbc
  jndi: java:comp/env/jdbc/rails_db
  driver: com.mysql.jdbc.Driver
```

The JRuby Extras project contains a set of database adapters for the most commonly used open source databases by Java developers, including h2, JavaDB (Derby), MySQL, HSQLDB (Hypersonic), and Postgres. The adapter gems give you the option of using ordinary Rails database configuration values in your *database.yml* file rather than specifying a class and JDBC driver URL. The gems also include and automatically load their respective JDBC driver JARs, so it isn't necessary to manually include the classes. If you are using one of the supported databases, you can install the gem by adding your database name, `mysql`, `postgres`, `derby`, `hsqldb`, or `h2` to the base gem name, `activerecord-jdbc`*<database name>*`-adapter`. This is how you would install the adapter for a MySQL database:

```
$ jruby -S gem install activerecord-jdbcmysql-adapter
```

This *database.yml* in Example 2-2 shows an example configuration that uses the newly installed gem. Notice how it doesn't use a JDBC URL as in the previous example, but uses standard Rails configuration parameters.

Example 2-2. Example database.yml using activerecord-jdbcmysql-adapter

```
development:
  adapter: jdbcmysql
  encoding: utf8
  database: jrubycookbook_development
  username: jruby
  password: cookbook
  port: 3306
  host: localhost
```

See Also

- Recipe 2.5, "Packaging Rails with a JNDI DataSource"
- The JRuby Extras Project, *http://rubyforge.org/projects/jruby-extras*

2.2 Packaging Rails As a Java EE Web Application

Problem

You want to package a Rails app as a Java EE web application for deployment onto a standard Java EE web container.

Solution

Use Warbler to package your Rails application as a WAR file. Start by installing the gem:

```
$ jruby -S gem install warbler
```

This gem adds the `warble` command, which allows you to create, configure, and clean up the WAR file. All Warbler commands should be executed in the root directory of your Rails application. Start by creating a Warbler configuration file with this command:

```
$ jruby -S warble config
```

The new configuration file is written to *config/warble.rb*. This file allows you to set most of the necessary options for building your WAR and determining how Rails will run in the web container. Open *warble.rb* and configure `config.webxml.rails.env` to the environment of your Rails deployment. Next, add all the gems used by your web application to the `config.gems` hash except for the `rails` gem. Rails is included in the default hash. An example *warble.rb* file showing these options can be seen in Example 2-3.

Example 2-3. Example Warbler configuration file

```
# Value of RAILS_ENV for the webapp
config.webxml.rails.env = 'development'

# List of all your application's gems
config.gems << "activerecord-jdbcmysql-adapter"
config.gems << "jruby-openssl"
```

You're ready to create a WAR file by running this command:

```
$ jruby -S warble war
```

This generates a WAR file named the Rails project home directory name by default. For example, if our Rails project was in the *MyKillerApplication* folder, the WAR file would be named *MyKillerApplication.war*. This WAR file can then be deployed into your Java EE container using the container's deployment process.

Discussion

Warbler is a Ruby gem for packaging a Rails application as a Java EE web application. It is built on the Rake build system and JRuby-Rack servlet adapter. The default implementation of the adapter uses a servlet filter that allows the container's default servlet to process the static content rather than Rails. Early versions of Warbler used the GoldSpike servlet, but the GoldSpike project has been deprecated and has been replaced by JRuby-Rack. The JRuby-Rack library includes a stub version of the GoldSpike servlet in order to maintain compatibility with legacy GoldSpike applications.

The unpacked source of the WAR file is found in the newly created *tmp/war* folder in the project's home directory. If you browse the contents of the unpacked WAR file, you'll see some parts of your Rails application mixed in with other familiar Java EE folders. Warbler reassembles the Rails application to the Java EE standard by placing the static content normally found in the Rails *public* folder in the top level of the WAR and packaging the rest of the Rails application in the *WEB-INF* directory. Warbler has also bundled *jruby-rack.jar*, which contains the necessary classes to integrate with a Java EE container, and *jruby-complete.jar*, the standalone distribution of the JRuby with all the dependent classes, in the *WEB-INF/lib* directory.

The `war` task is actually comprised of many subtasks, which you can access separately. Since Warbler is a wrapper around Rake, use the `-T` flag to see a full list of Warbler's options and description of its capabilities:

```
$ jruby -S warble -T
rake config              # Generate a configuration file to customize your wa...
rake pluginize           # Unpack warbler as a plugin in your Rails application
rake version             # Display version of warbler
rake war                 # Create MyKillerApplication.war
rake war:app             # Copy all application files into the .war
rake war:clean           # Clean up the .war file and the staging area
rake war:gems            # Unpack all gems into WEB-INF/gems
rake war:jar             # Run the jar command to create the .war
rake war:java_classes    # Copy java classes into the .war
rake war:java_libs       # Copy all java libraries into the .war
rake war:public          # Copy all public HTML files to the root of the .war
rake war:webxml          # Generate a web.xml file for the webapp
```

By default, Warbler will include the latest version of each gem in your gem repository, but you have the option to target specific versions of gems when packaging the WAR file. Set the `config.gems` hash with the version number of the gem like this:

```
config.gems["rails"] = "2.0.2"
config.gems["activerecord-jdbcmysql-adapter"] = "0.8.2"
```

See Also

• Recipe 2.1, "Installing and Setting Up Rails"

2.3 Using an External Gem Repository with a Web Application

Problem

You don't want to package your gems into your web application but want to use a gem repository on the filesystem.

Solution

There are a few situations where you might want to use a different gem repository outside of the default JRuby runtime's repository. This could useful when you are maintaining a shared set of gems that are being accessed by both C Ruby and JRuby. You can configure your web application to use a separate gem repository through the `gem.path` or `gem.home` system properties. These properties can be set in the WAR's descriptor file, *web.xml*, or through a system property when the container is started, as seen in Example 2-4.

Example 2-4. Sample web.xml setting the gem.path context parameter

```
<context-param>
    <param-name>gem.path</param-name>
    <param-value>C:\projects\jruby\jruby-1.1\lib\ruby\gems</param-value>
</context-param>

<!-- Alternatively
<context-param>
    <param-name>gem.home</param-name>
    <param-value>C:\projects\jruby\jruby-1.1\lib\ruby\gems</param-value>
</context-param>-->
```

You can also set the `gem.path` in the startup parameters for the servlet container:

```
$ java -jar start.jar etc/jetty.xml \
-Dgem.path="C:\projects\jruby\jruby-1.1\lib\ruby\gems"
```

See Also

- Recipe 2.2, "Packaging Rails As a Java EE Web Application"

2.4 Configuring the JRuby-Rack Servlet

Problem

You want to configure the number of JRuby runtimes in the container.

Solution

Edit the values in *warble.rb* to your desired settings:

```
config.webxml.jruby.min.runtimes = 2
config.webxml.jruby.max.runtimes = 4
```

Generate the Rails WAR file:

```
$ jruby -S warble war
```

Discussion

The JRuby-Rack servlet allows Rails to integrate into most Java EE containers. Because many parts of Rails prior to version 2.2 are not threadsafe, the runtime cannot be used to simultaneously process multiple requests. JRuby-Rack utilizes a configurable pool of JRuby runtimes that are dispatched for each incoming Rails request. The number of simultaneous requests that can be processed is limited by the number of available runtimes. Any additional requests will block and must wait for a runtime to become free. It's highly advised that you set a maximum number of runtimes for your production application because by default Warbler will allow for an unlimited number of runtimes. These are all the configuration options:

`config.webxml.jruby.max.runtimes`

> This sets the most number of active JRuby runtimes in the pool, which determines the maximum number of simultaneous requests. Default value is unlimited.

`config.webxml.jruby.min.runtimes`

> This determines the number of "warm" runtimes or the minimum number of runtimes in the pool. It also dictates how many instances when the application is started. The default value is none.

`config.webxml.jruby.runtime.initializer.threads`

> This sets how many threads will be used to initialize the JRuby runtimes in the pool. The value will vary based on the number of runtimes you intend to use at startup and the initialization time of the pool. The default value is 4.

`config.webxml.jruby.runtime.timeout.sec`

> This sets how long in milliseconds an incoming request should wait for a JRuby runtime before returning an error. The default is 30 seconds.

The CPU, memory, and system resources of the host machine generally determine the number of maximum and minimum idle runtimes. The JRuby runtime is a memory-intensive application, so it is recommended to run the application with a generous amount of both permanent generation (PermGen) and heap memory. This is especially true when using a large number of runtimes.

> Developers who are upgrading from an early version of Warbler and using the GoldSpike servlet can continue to use their existing *warble.rb* file to configure the JRuby pools. The JRuby-Rack adapter supports the legacy GoldSpike configuration values, but you're advised to update your configuration to JRuby-Rack parameters because it's possible this support will be eliminated in later releases.

See Also

- Recipe 2.2, "Packaging Rails As a Java EE Web Application"

2.5 Packaging Rails with a JNDI DataSource

Problem

You want to configure your Rails application to access a JDBC DataSource through Java Naming and Directory Interface (JNDI).

Solution

Install the `activerecord-jdbc-adapter` gem (as in Recipe 2.1) and edit your *database.yml* file. The JNDI lookup service is provided by the `jdbc` adapter gem. Set the `driver` value to your database's JDBC `Driver` class and add the JNDI location of the JDBC DataSource. This example *database.yml* file is configured to use a JDBC factory for a MySQL database:

```
development:
  adapter: jdbc
  jndi: java:comp/env/jdbc/rails_db
  driver: com.mysql.jdbc.Driver
```

Use Warbler to package your Rails application (see Recipe 2.2). Edit your *warble.rb* file and set the resource reference name of your JNDI DataSource in the configuration file:

```
# JNDI data source name
config.webxml.jndi = 'jdbc/rails_db'
```

Repackage the WAR by running Warbler's `war` task:

```
$ jruby -S warble war
```

Discussion

The `war` or `war:webxml` tasks create or overwrite an existing Java EE web deployment descriptor file, */WEB-INF/web.xml*, in your Warbler staging area, *tmp/war*. Both tasks add the `resource-ref` definition and all the required information for a new JDBC DataSource. Here is an example *web.xml* for Rails application using a JNDI DataSource referenced at `jdbc/rails_db`:

```
<resource-ref>
    <res-ref-name>jdbc/rails_db</res-ref-name>
    <res-type>javax.sql.DataSource</res-type>
    <res-auth>Container</res-auth>
</resource-ref>
```

You always have the option of manually editing the files and values generated by Warbler. If you choose to edit the *web.xml* descriptor file by defining new DataSources or setting configuration values or references, you can use Warbler's `war:jar` task to skip the file generation steps and package all the files in the staging folder into the application WAR file:

```
$ jruby -S warble war:jar
```

See Also

- Recipe 2.2, "Packaging Rails As a Java EE Web Application"

2.6 Deploying Rails on Tomcat

Problem

You want to deploy a Rails Java EE application using Apache Tomcat.

Solution

Package your Rails application as a Java EE WAR (see Recipe 2.2). Place the resulting WAR file in the Tomcat's *webapps* directory. If you are using one of the database-specific JDBC adapter gems, you're ready to start Tomcat. If your Rails application is using the regular `jdbc` adapter, include the JDBC adapter's JAR file in your classpath or copy the JAR file into *$TOMCAT_HOME/common/lib*.

Be sure to set the `JAVA_HOME` environment variable to the folder where you've installed Java. A performance tip is to start Tomcat with the `-server` flag. It is also advisable to set constraints for the heap and PermGen so potential memory leaks do not consume all the resources on the server and cripple the machine.

Windows

```
> set JAVA_HOME=c:\Program Files\Java\jdk1.5.0_12
> set CATALINA_OPTS=-server -Xms512m -Xmx1024m -XX:PermSize=256m \
  -XX:MaxPermSize=512m
> catalina.bat start
```

Linux and OS X

```
$ export JAVA_HOME=/usr/java/jdk1.5.0_12
$ export CATALINA_OPTS='-server -Xms512m -Xmx1024m -XX:PermSize=256m
  -XX:MaxPermSize=512m'
$ ./catalina.sh start
```

Discussion

 It is important to understand JRuby's memory usage so that you can properly tune your applications. The JVM has separate memory spaces. One, known as permanent generation (PermGen), is reserved for internal class file representations and VM data structures. The other, heap, is the more commonly known and is typically used to store the data represented in those classes. A lot of JRuby success is owed to the ability to work around the rules of a statically compiled language (i.e., Java) by generating classes and data structures at runtime. The cost of this approach is that in some cases JRuby may need to generate a large number of objects and these objects are all stored in the permanent generation space and not the heap. Consider the case of Rails, where a single request could generate hundreds of JRuby objects. This usage of PermGen is many times the default case, so the default VM memory setting is often insufficient. The JRuby team has made strides in alleviating the problem, such as allowing JRuby runtimes to share PermGen space, but you should take a cautious approach by setting initial and maximum values for your PermGen and heap, especially for production applications.

If you are using Tomcat with a JNDI DataSource, then start by packaging your Rails application (see Recipe 2.2). Navigate to the WAR's staging area, *tmp/war*, and add the *context.xml* file to the *META-INF* folder. Create the folder if it does not already exist. Example 2-5 shows how you would define a resource in *context.xml* to access a MySQL database. The resource definition includes the database connection information, the resource's JNDI name, and the context path of this application, which will match the beginning of the request Uniform Resource Identifier (URI) of your web application.

Example 2-5. Tomcat context.xml JNDI configuration

```
<Context path="/MyKillerApplication" docBase="MyKillerApplication"
        debug="5" reloadable="true" crossContext="true">

    <Resource name="jdbc/rails_db" auth="Container" type="javax.sql.DataSource"
            maxActive="100" maxIdle="30" maxWait="10000"
            username="root" password="password"
            driverClassName="com.mysql.jdbc.Driver"
url="jdbc:mysql://localhost:3306/jrubycookbook_development?autoReconnect=true"/>

</Context>
```

The resource could have also been defined in *$TOMCAT_HOME/conf/server.xml*, but that approach is discouraged by the Tomcat authors since it applies to all the web applications. Packaging the resource in the web application makes sense both because it reflects good code organization and because it allows you to redefine and update the DataSource by redeploying the self-contained web application and avoid restarting the server.

Rebuild the WAR using `warble`, move your application to the deployment folder, and start the server using the information provided in the solution.

See Also

- Recipe 2.2, "Packaging Rails As a Java EE Web Application"
- Recipe 2.5, "Packaging Rails with a JNDI DataSource"

2.7 Deploying Rails on JBoss

Problem

You want to deploy a Rails application on the JBoss Application Server.

Solution

Package your Rails application as a Java EE WAR (see Recipe 2.2). Copy the application WAR into *$JBOSS_HOME\server\default\deploy*, the default JBoss deployment folder, or any server-specific deployment directory you have defined in the JBoss configuration files. If you are using the non-database-specific `jdbc` adapter for connecting to your database, be sure to include the JDBC JAR in the classpath. You can also copy the JDBC JAR into *$JBOSS_HOME\server\default\lib* if you're running the default server.

Be sure to start the application server with the `-server` flag and set some expected size for your heap and permanent generation, PermGen, memory space. Typically this is done through the `JAVA_OPTS` environment variable.

Windows

```
> SET JAVA_HOME=c:\Program Files\Java\jdk1.5.0_12
> SET JAVA_OPTS=-server –Xms512m –Xmx1024m -XX:PermSize=256m –XX:MaxPermSize=512m
> run.bat
```

Linux and OS X

```
$ export JAVA_HOME=/usr/java/jdk1.5.0_12
$ export JAVA_OPTS='-server –Xms512m –Xmx1024m -XX:PermSize=256m\
  –XX:MaxPermSize=512m'
$ ./run.sh
```

Discussion

If you are using a JNDI resource for your Rails database connection, you will need to create the DataSource in the JBoss server. The JBoss distribution provides sample DataSource configurations for most of the popular databases in the examples folder, *$JBOSS_HOME\docs\examples\jca*. This a great starting place for simple database setups. After you have edited the file, you can easily deploy a DataSource in JBoss by placing the file in the deployment directory. *$JBOSS_HOME\server\default\deploy* is the deployment folder for the default server.

If you're running a MySQL database, change the `<jndi-name>MySqlDS</jndi-name>` configuration parameter to the name of your DataSource, `rails_db` in this example. Set the rest of database information in the configuration file with the appropriate values for your database. Example 2-6 shows an edited *mysql-ds.xml* DataSource definition for the example application. Note that the `jndi-name` does not include the `jdbc` prefix. Copy the *mysql-ds.xml* file to your deployment directory.

Example 2-6. Sample mysql-ds.xml JBoss DataSource configuration file

```
<datasources>
  <local-tx-datasource>
    <jndi-name>rails_db</jndi-name>
    <connection-url>
       jdbc:mysql://localhost:3306/jrubycookbook_development
    </connection-url>
    <driver-class>com.mysql.jdbc.Driver</driver-class>
    <user-name>root</user-name>
    <password>password</password>
    <connection-property name="autoReconnect">true</connection-property>
    <!-- Typemapping for JBoss 4.0 -->
    <metadata>
      <type-mapping>mySQL</type-mapping>
    </metadata>
  </local-tx-datasource>
</datasources>
```

Even though you have defined the DataSource, you still need to map between this resource and the web application. This binding information is defined in the *jboss-web.xml* file and packaged along with your web application. Warbler does not generate this file, so you will need to create the *jboss-web.xml* file in the *WEB-INF* directory of Warbler's staging area, *tmp/war*, as in Example 2-7.

Example 2-7. Sample JBoss deployment descriptor

```
<jboss-web>
    <context-root>/MyKillerApplication</context-root>
    <resource-ref>
        <res-ref-name>jdbc/rails_db</res-ref-name>
        <res-type>javax.sql.DataSource</res-type>
        <jndi-name>java:rails_db</jndi-name>
    </resource-ref>
</jboss-web>
```

You can configure your DataSource to be the default DataSource for the JBoss server by naming it `DefaultDS` and removing the default DataSource included with the JBoss installation, *$JBOSS_HOME/server/all/deploy/hsqldb-ds.xml*.

See Also

- Recipe 2.2, "Packaging Rails As a Java EE Web Application"
- Recipe 2.5, "Packaging Rails with a JNDI DataSource"

2.8 Deploying Rails on Jetty

Problem

You want to deploy a Rails application on the Jetty Servlet container.

Solution

Package your Rails application as a Java EE WAR (see Recipe 2.2). If you've defined a JDBC connection with the **jdbc** adapter or using a JNDI DataSource, remember to include the JDBC adapter in your classpath or copy the JAR into *$JETTY_HOME/lib* to make it available to any deployed web applications. Place the WAR into Jetty's *$JETTY_HOME/webapp* folder. Start the server with the **-server** VM option and default heap and PermGen values:

```
$ java -server -Xms512m -Xmx1024m -XX:PermSize=256m -XX:MaxPermSize=512m\
    -jar start.jar etc/jetty.xml
```

Discussion

If you would like to use a JNDI resource for your Rails database connection, start by defining a DataSource in your WAR. Create a file called *jetty-env.xml* in the *WEB-INF* folder of your staging area. Example 2-8 shows a *jetty-env.xml* configuration for a MySQL database.

Example 2-8. Sample jetty-env.xml file

```
<?xml version="1.0"?>
<!DOCTYPE Configure PUBLIC "-//Mort Bay Consulting//DTD Configure//EN"
 "http://jetty.mortbay.org/configure.dtd">

<Configure class="org.mortbay.jetty.webapp.WebAppContext">

  <New id="rails_db" class="org.mortbay.jetty.plus.naming.Resource">
    <Arg>jdbc/rails_db</Arg>
    <Arg>
      <New class="com.mysql.jdbc.jdbc2.optional.MysqlConnectionPoolDataSource">
        <Set name="Url">jdbc:mysql://localhost:3306/jrubycookbook_development</Set>
        <Set name="User">root</Set>
        <Set name="Password">password</Set>
      </New>
    </Arg>
  </New>
</Configure>
```

Repackage your application with Warbler and deploy to Jetty. Jetty's JNDI module is not enabled in the standard *webapps* deployment folder by default, so either update *$JETTY_HOME/etc/jetty.xml* to enable JNDI for this directory or configure Jetty to use an alternative directory. It is the Jetty convention to install applications that require JNDI into the *webapps-plus* directory:

```
$ copy MyKillerApplication.war $JETTY_HOME/webapps-plus
```

Jetty supplies a convenient *$JETTY_HOME/etc/jetty-plus.xml* file, which configures Jetty to use that folder. Run this command from the Jetty home directory to start Jetty with JNDI support:

```
$ java -server -Xms512m -Xmx1024m -XX:PermSize=256m -XX:MaxPermSize=512m -jar\
  start.jar etc/jetty.xml etc/jetty-plus.xml
```

See Also

- Recipe 2.2, "Packaging Rails As a Java EE Web Application"
- Recipe 2.5, "Packaging Rails with a JNDI DataSource"

2.9 Deploying Rails with jetty_rails

Problem

Many Rails developers today have never worked with the Java EE packaging process and launch their applications by navigating to the top level of their Rails project and starting one of two popular Ruby web servers: Mongrel or WEBrick. You want to run the Jetty application server with your Rails application but use a deployment method more familiar to Rails developers.

Solution

Use the `jetty_rails` gem, which allows you to run a Rails application with the Jetty server without performing any Java EE packaging. First, install the `jetty_rails` gem:

```
jruby -S gem install jetty_rails
```

Then, go to the top of your Rails application and start the Jetty server:

```
$ cd jrubycook_application
$ jruby -S jetty_rails
```

Discussion

You can get a list of some common startup parameters by running this command:

```
jruby -S jetty_rails --help
```

The `port` and `environment` options are common startup parameters used in the Mongrel and WEBrick HTTP servers:

- Pass in the `--port <port>` or `-p <port>` parameter to set the port of your web application. The default is 3000.

- Use the `--environment <env>` or `-e <env>` to specify the Rails execution environment. The default value is `development`.

- Set the `--context-path <path>` or `-u <path>` parameter to change your applications context root. Remember to make your Rails application aware of this change by adding this line of code to your *environment.rb* file:

  ```
  ActionController::AbstractRequest.relative_url_root = "/my_new_context_root"
  ```

- Use the `-c` or `--config` parameter to load the server configuration through an external file. The server will look in the default location, *config/jetty_rails.yml*, if you do not include a file path.

The configuration file is valuable beyond the organizational benefit of getting the start-up parameters out of the input arguments. As of version 0.6, you can use the file to tune your application by setting JRuby and Jetty configuration values, leverage a powerful layered configuration system, and run multiple Rails applications within a single Jetty instance.

Example 2-9 demonstrates some of these features by configuring several Rails applications, each in its own context, through individual **content_path** definitions as well as a **port** definition. The default parameters are set at the end of the file and optionally overridden within the configuration section for each application. Note in the example how the development applications override the number of initial runtimes from five to two.

Example 2-9. Sample jetty_rails.xml configuration file

```
---
:servers:
- :context_path: /dev-one
  :adapter: :rails
  :environment: development
  :base: development-dir
  :port: 3000
  :jruby_initial_runtimes: 2
- :context_path: /prod-one
  :adapter: :rails
  :base: production-dir
- :port: 4000
  :apps:
  - :context_path: /dev-two
    :adapter: :rails
    :base: development-dir
    :environment: development
    :jruby_initial_runtimes: 2
  - :context_path: /prod-two
    :base: production-dir
    :adapter: :rails
:environment: production
```

```
:jruby_initial_runtimes: 5
:jruby_max_runtimes: 10
:thread_pool_min: 5
:thread_pool_max: 40
:acceptor_size: 20
```

These are some of the less familiar configuration options:

jruby_initial_runtimes
> Specifies the number of JRuby runtimes that will be created on startup. Note that there are separate runtime pools for each application context.

jruby_max_runtimes
> Sets the maximum number of runtimes in the pool and limits the number of simultaneous Rails requests.

thread_pool_min
> Sets the initial size of the pool of request-handling threads.

thread_pool_max
> Sets the maximum size of the pool of request-handling threads.

acceptor_size
> Sets the number of acceptors for Jetty's Java NIO-based `SelectChannelConnector`.

See Also

- Jetty-Rails website, *http://jetty-rails.rubyforge.org*

2.10 Deploying Rails with Mongrel

Problem

You want to run a JRuby on Rails application with Mongrel.

Solution

Install the Mongrel gem. The JRuby gem installer should select the latest Java version of the gem:

```
$ jruby -S gem install mongrel --no-ri --no-rdoc
Updating metadata for 165 gems from http://gems.rubyforge.org
...............................................................
complete
Successfully installed gem_plugin-0.2.3
Successfully installed mongrel-1.1.4-java
2 gems installed
```

Include the JDBC adapter of your database in your classpath if you aren't using the database-specific `jdbc` adapter that packages and loads the driver. Go to your Rails application's home directory and start Mongrel:

```
$ jruby -S mongrel_rails start
** Starting Mongrel listening at 0.0.0.0:3000
** Starting Rails with development environment...
** Rails loaded.
** Loading any Rails specific GemPlugins
** Signals ready.  TERM => stop.  USR2 => restart.  INT => stop (no restart).
** Rails signals registered.  HUP => reload (without restart).  It might not wor
k well.
** Mongrel 1.1.4 available at 0.0.0.0:3000
** Use CTRL-C to stop.
```

Discussion

Mongrel is a small but high-performance web server originally written in Ruby and C. Recently, the C portions have been ported to Java so that Mongrel can run under JRuby. This was an important milestone for the project given that many Rails developers use Mongrel in their production and development environments.

There is an experimental gem to provide clustering support for the Java version of Mongrel called `mongrel_jcluster`. Unfortunately, this gem is currently only supported on Linux, OS X, and Cygwin on Windows. The default Windows DOS shell is currently not yet supported. This gem allows you easily start and stop sets of Mongrel servers and attempts to recreate some of the functionality of `mongrel_cluster`, which is incompatible with JRuby. First, install the gem:

```
$ jruby -S gem install mongrel_jcluster
Successfully installed mongrel_jcluster-0.0.1
1 gem installed
```

Next, generate a configuration file for your Mongrel cluster:

```
$ jruby -S mongrel_rails jcluster::configure -p 4000 -N 3 -e development -R 20202\
  -K thesecretkey
Writing configuration file to config/mongrel_jcluster.yml.
```

The new file in *config/mongrel_jcluster.yml* allows you to set the starting port number of the servers of the -p flag, the number of instances with -N, and the runtime environment of the cluster with the -e flag.

Start your Mongrel cluster with this command:

```
$ jruby -S mongrel_rails jcluster::start
Starting JRuby server...
Starting 3 Mongrel servers...
```

Open your browser to *http://localhost:4000*, *http://localhost:4001*, and *http://localhost: 4002* to verify that your cluster has properly started. You can stop the cluster with this command:

```
$ jruby -S mongrel_rails jcluster::stop
Stopping 3 Mongrel servers...
```

2.11 Deploying Rails on the GlassFish v2 Server

Problem

You want to deploy a Rails application on the GlassFish v2 application server.

Solution

Install the GlassFish server and navigate to the home directory. Set up the deployment area and configure the server with the supplied ant task:

```
$ $GLASSFISH_HOME/lib/ant/bin/ant -f setup.xml
```

This will install several libraries and create your Java EE application deployment folder at *$GLASSFISH_HOME\domains\domain1\autodeploy*. Package your Rails application as a Java EE WAR (see Recipe 2.2). If you've defined a JDBC connection with the **jdbc** adapter or using a JNDI DataSource, remember to include the JDBC adapter in your classpath or copy the JAR file into *$GLASSFISH_HOME/lib* to make it available to your web applications.

Start the server with this command:

```
$ $GLASSFISH_HOME/bin/asadmin start-domain
```

Wait a few seconds after the server starts to allow enough time to deploy your Rails WAR (Figure 2-2).

Figure 2-2. Starting up the GlassFish server

Open your browser to *http://localhost:8080/MyKillerApplication* to view your Rails project.

Discussion

Rails applications that use a JNDI DataSource can use the `asadmin` command with input parameters to define the DataSource's properties. This example creates a connection pool for a MySQL server at our standard example address `jdbc/rails_db`:

```
$ $GLASSFISH_HOME\bin\asadmin create-jdbc-connection-pool -datasourceclassname \
  com.mysql.jdbc.jdbc2.optional.MysqlConnectionPoolDataSource \
  --restype javax.sql.DataSource -property User=root:Password=password:\
  URL=jdbc\:mysql\://localhost:3316/jrubycookbook_development jdbc/rails_db
Command create-jdbc-connection-pool executed successfully.
```

Next, make the new DataSource available to your Rails WAR and other Java EE applications installed on the server:

```
$ $GLASSFISH_HOME\bin\asadmin create-jdbc-resource --connectionpoolid \
  jdbc/rails_db jdbc/rails_db
Command create-jdbc-resource executed successfully.
```

See Also

* Recipe 2.12, "Using the GlassFish v3 Gem"

2.12 Using the GlassFish v3 Gem

Problem

You want to run a Rails application with the GlassFish v3 gem.

Solution

First, install the GlassFish v3 gem:

```
$ jruby -S gem install glassfish
  Successfully installed glassfish-0.1.2-universal-java
  1 gem installed
```

Start your Rails application with the new `glassfish_rails` command. You currently have to start the server in the directory that contains your Rails application directory:[*]

```
$ jruby -S glassfish_rails MyKillerApplication
```

Open your browser to *http://localhost:3000* and you should see the Rails welcome screen.

---

[*] It is likely this will be changed in future releases.

Discussion

The GlassFish v3 server is Sun's latest effort to build a widely adopted Java EE server. They have packaged this server as a Ruby gem and configured it to run Rails with a few simple commands.

The gem implements a pool of JRuby runtimes that work a lot like the pooling used in the GoldSpike servlet. You can set the number of JRuby runtimes in the pool by using the –n or the --runtimes flag when starting the server. The following examples will start up servers with three runtimes in each pool:

```
$ jruby –S glassfish_rails MyKillerApplication –n 3
```

or:

```
$ jruby –S glassfish_rails MyKillerApplication --runtimes 3
```

See Also

- Recipe 2.11, "Deploying Rails on the GlassFish v2 Server"

2.13 Using ActiveRecord Outside of Rails

Problem

You want to use ActiveRecord as the Object-Relational Mapping (ORM) solution for a non-Rails application.

Solution

If you have not installed Rails, install the activerecord gem:

```
$ jruby -S gem install activerecord --no-ri --no-rdoc
```

Install the activerecord-jdbc-adapter gem, which will provide access to the database through a JDBC connection:

```
$ jruby -S gem install activerecord-jdbc-adapter --no-ri --no-rdoc
```

Include your database's JDBC adapter in your classpath or JRuby *lib* folder if you're not using a database-specific adapter. For example, to connect to a MySQL database, you will need the activerecord-jdbcmysql-adapter gem. See Recipe 2.1 for more information about database-specific drivers and gems.

```
$ jruby -S gem install activerecord-jdbcmysql-adapter --no-ri --no-rdoc
```

Create a YAML file called *database.yml* such as the one in Example 2-10 to define your database connection parameters.

Example 2-10. Sample database.yml file

```
development:
  adapter: jdbcmysql
  database: jrubycookbook_development
  host: localhost
  port: 3306
  username: root
  password: password
```

Once this setup is in place, you can load the file and establish a connection to one of the databases defined in it. In Example 2-11, we load the **development** database defined in the configuration file from Example 2-10. Once the database connection has been established, we run a query and iterate through the results. Finally, we utilize one of the dynamic finder methods that are attached to objects by the ActiveRecord framework.

Example 2-11. Loading a database.yml file and accessing the database

```
require 'rubygems'
gem 'activerecord-jdbcmysql-adapter'
require 'active_record'
require 'yaml'

@connections = YAML.load_file("database.yml")
ActiveRecord::Base.establish_connection(@connections["development"])

stmt = "select id, title from games"
@val = ActiveRecord::Base.connection.select_all(stmt)
@val.each do |g|
     puts "game id: #{g["id"]} #{g["title"]}"
end

class Game < ActiveRecord::Base
end

puts "found game id: #{Game.find(1).id}"
```

This is the output of the program:

```
$ jruby games.rb
game id: 1 Alien Invasion
looking up game id: 1
```

Discussion

JRuby's `jirb` interactive console is a wonderful environment to prototype and test application code. Running `jirb` with our example program gives you an interactive session with the database (Figure 2-3).

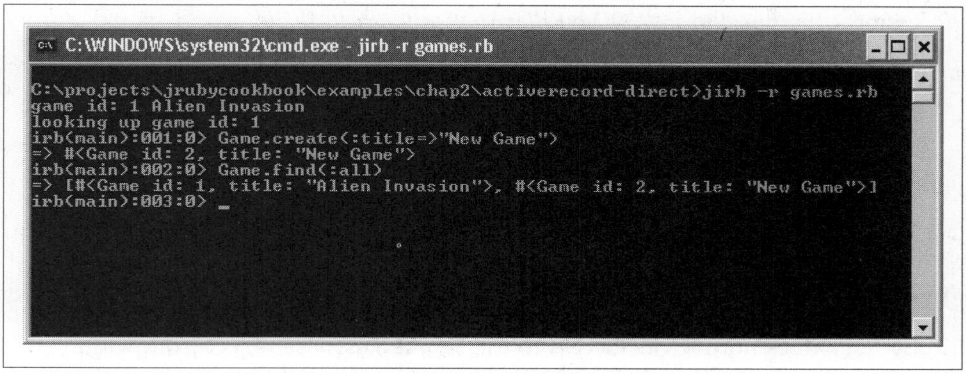

Figure 2-3. jirb session using ActiveRecord and a JDBC connection

2.14 Accessing Common Java Servlet Information

Problem

You want to access the Java servlet request object from your Rails controllers.

Solution

JRuby-Rack's servlet filter makes several servlet variables available to the Rails application on each incoming request. Access the standard **javax.servlet.ServletRequest** through the Rack environment map with the key **java.servlet_request**. The **Servlet Context** object can also be fetched through the Rack environment hash with the **java.servlet_context** key, or through the global variable, **$servlet_context**. Example 2-12 shows a controller that uses some of these variables.

Example 2-12. Accessing the Java servlet objects from a Rails controller

```
class HelloWorldController < ApplicationController
    def hello
      ctx = request.env['java.servlet_context']
      puts "server info: #{ctx.server_info}"
      puts "server info: #{$servlet_context.server_info}"

      req = request.env['java.servlet_request']
      puts "uri: #{req.request_uri}"
      puts "query string: #{req.query_string}"
      puts "port: #{req.server_port}"
      puts "param hello: #{req.get_parameter("hello")}"
      puts "session id: #{req.get_session.id}"
    end
end
```

Accessing *http://localhost:3000/MyKillerApplication/hello?hello=world* would output these messages to the container's log file:

```
server info: jetty-6.1.9
server info: jetty-6.1.9
uri: /hello_world/hello
query string: hello=world
port: 3000
param hello: world
session id: 2026
```

Discussion

JRuby-Rack does not provide access to the `ServletResponse` object from within your controller. This feature was available in earlier versions of Warbler through the Gold-Spike servlet but has been removed after the integration of JRuby-Rack.

See Also

- Recipe 2.4, "Configuring the JRuby-Rack Servlet"

2.15 Configuring Session Storage

Problem

You want to configure the session storage mechanism used by your Rails application.

Solution

Edit the *web.xml* file in your web application and set the `jruby.session_store` context parameter to `db` by adding this bit of code:

```
<context-param>
        <param-name>jruby.session_store</param-name>
        <param-value>db</param-value>
        <!-- This value really means let Rails take care of session store -->
</context-param>
```

Discussion

By default, JRuby-Rack's servlet filter uses the Java EE servlet container's session storage. Changing the `jruby.session_store` context parameter to `db` tells JRuby-Rack to defer to Rails's session management.

See Also

- Recipe 2.2, "Packaging Rails As a Java EE Web Application"

2.16 Controlling the Classes, Directories, and Other Files Packaged into a Rails WAR File

Problem

There are classes and other files you want to include and/or exclude from your WAR file.

Solution

Open the Warbler configuration file *config/warbler.rb* and validate these configuration options:

```
# Application directories to be included in the webapp.
config.dirs = %w(app config lib log vendor tmp)

# Additional files/directories to include, above those in config.dirs
config.includes = FileList["db"]

# Additional files/directories to exclude
config.excludes = FileList["lib/tasks/*"]

# Additional Java .jar files to include.  Note that if .jar files are placed
# in lib (and not otherwise excluded) then they need not be mentioned here
# JRuby and JRuby-Rack are pre-loaded in this list.
# Be sure to include your own versions if you directly set the value
config.java_libs += FileList["lib/java/*.jar"]

# Loose Java classes and miscellaneous files to be placed in WEB-INF/classes.
config.java_classes = FileList["target/classes/**.*"]

# One or more pathmaps defining how the java classes should be copied into
# WEB-INF/classes. The example pathmap below accompanies the java_classes
# configuration above. See http://rake.rubyforge.org/classes/String.html#M000017
# for details of how to specify a pathmap.
config.pathmaps.java_classes << "%{target/classes/,}"
```

Discussion

By default, Warbler will include the JRuby runtime and JRuby-Rack in the WAR files it produces. There are some cases where you might prefer to install these JARs in a shared library area rather than packaging the JAR files with each web application. The shared packaging approach can accomplish this, but some developers may want a mixed approach, in which the packaged WAR file includes dependent gems but not the JRuby runtime and the JRuby-Rack servlet. The `config.java_libs` property is simply a Ruby array, so you can use well-known array operations to exclude items from Warbler's build process. For example, you can use the `reject!` method with a regular expression to exclude all versions of JRuby and JRuby-Rack from the final WAR file:

```
config.java_libs.reject! {|lib| lib =~ /jruby-complete|jruby-rack/ }
```

If you're changing these configuration values, it is recommended that you run Warbler's `war:clean` task between builds to prevent files from being accidentally included into your WAR. This is especially the case if you are experimenting with the exclusion rules.

See Also

- Recipe 2.2, "Packaging Rails As a Java EE Web Application"

2.17 Changing the Name of the WAR File and the Staging Area

Problem

You want to change the name of the WAR file and/or Warbler's staging area.

Solution

By default, Warbler will name the generated WAR file according to the Rails application's directory name. You can customize the name by setting the `config.war_name` parameter in your *config/warbler.rb* configuration file:

```
# Name of the war file (without the .war) -- defaults to the basename
# of RAILS_ROOT
config.war_name = "mywar"
```

You may also want to modify the staging folder that contains the decompressed source files for the final WAR. In *warbler.rb*, set the `config.staging_dir` to your target staging folder:

```
# Temporary directory where the application is staged
config.staging_dir = "tmp/war"
```

See Also

- Recipe 2.2, "Packaging Rails As a Java EE Web Application"
- Recipe 2.18, "Deploying a Rails Application to the Root Context"

2.18 Deploying a Rails Application to the Root Context

Problem

You want to make your Java EE web application available from the root context of the servlet container.

Solution

In general, the simplest approach is to package your Rails application with the name *ROOT.war*. This can be configured using the Warbler configuration file, *warble.rb*:

```
config.war_name = "ROOT"
```

Before deploying this WAR file, be sure to remove any existing directories named *ROOT* or *ROOT.war* files from your container's deployment directories.

Discussion

Although not actually part of the Java EE standard, using a filename of *ROOT.war* to indicate to the servlet container that you want this application to be deployed in the root context is a widely used convention. Each container defines a custom deployment descriptor. We've seen examples of these descriptors in previous recipes. If you are using JNDI DataSources, you will need to modify the deployment descriptors to match the context name.

Tomcat

Edit the *context.xml* file in the *META-INF* directory in your staging area (see Recipe 2.7). Set the `path` and `docBase` attributes to / (Example 2-13). Warbler does not create this file by default so you will have to create it yourself and repackage the WAR.

Example 2-13. Changing the context path for a Tomcat deployment

```
<Context path="/" docBase="/" debug="5" reloadable="true" crossContext="true">

    <Resource name="jdbc/rails_db" auth="Container" type="javax.sql.DataSource"
              maxActive="100" maxIdle="30" maxWait="10000"
              username="root" password="password"
              driverClassName="com.mysql.jdbc.Driver"
url="jdbc:mysql://localhost:3306/jrubycookbook_development?autoReconnect=true"/>

</Context>
```

JBoss

Edit the *jboss-web.xml* file in the *WEB-INF* directory in your staging area (see Recipe 2.8). Change the `context-root` value to / (Example 2-14). Warbler does not create this file by default so you will have to create it yourself and repackage the WAR.

Example 2-14. Changing the context path for a JBoss deployment

```
<jboss-web>
    <context-root>/</context-root>
    <resource-ref>
        <res-ref-name>jdbc/rails_db</res-ref-name>
        <res-type>javax.sql.DataSource</res-type>
        <jndi-name>java:rails_db</jndi-name>
```

```
      </resource-ref>
</jboss-web>
```

Jetty

Edit the *jetty-web.xml* file in the *WEB-INF* directory in your staging area (see Recipe 2.9). Add the configuration in Example 2-15. Warbler does not create this file by default so you will have to create it yourself and repackage the WAR.

Example 2-15. Changing the context path for a Jetty deployment

```
<?xml version="1.0" encoding="ISO-8859-1"?>
<!DOCTYPE Configure PUBLIC "-//Mort Bay Consulting//DTD Configure//EN"
 "http://jetty.mortbay.org/configure.dtd">
<Configure class="org.mortbay.jetty.webapp.WebAppContext">
  <Set name="contextPath">/</Set>
</Configure>
```

No configuration changes are necessary to allow Jetty to find your JNDI DataSource.

See Also

- Recipe 2.6, "Deploying Rails on Tomcat"
- Recipe 2.7, "Deploying Rails on JBoss"
- Recipe 2.8, "Deploying Rails on Jetty"
- Recipe 2.17, "Changing the Name of the WAR File and the Staging Area"

2.19 Creating a Rails Application with Aptana Studio

Problem

You want to create a Rails application using Aptana Studio.

Solution

Download and install the Aptana Studio software from the Aptana website, *http://www .aptana.com/download*. Open the Aptana start page at Help→Aptana Studio Start Page and scroll to the RadRails information in the Plugins column. Click on the Install button on the start page and complete the installation wizard. You can also install the plugin by selecting the RadRails item in the Plugin Manager, located in a tab in the bottom frame, and clicking on the installation icon. Both options are shown in Figure 2-4.

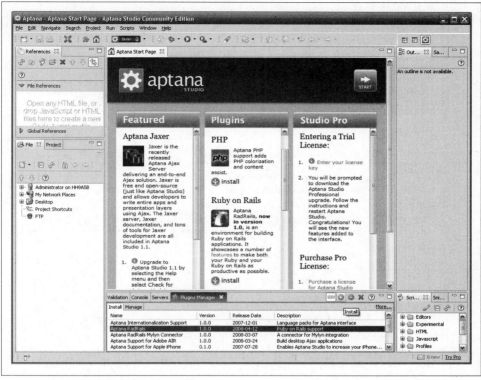

Figure 2-4. Aptana Studio: RadRails installation options

Aptana is built on the Eclipse IDE platform. As a result, the solution from Recipe 1.11 should be followed to set up the JRuby runtime and other common Eclipse configuration options. Once configuration is complete, choose the RadRails perspective by clicking on the new RadRails icon or select Other→RadRails in the perspectives menu in the top right corner of the window. Create your new Rails application by selecting File→New→Rails Project in the menu. Give the project a name and choose your database platform from the available options. Click Finish, and RadRails will generate the files for your Rails application, which are shown in the left Rails File Explorer window. The default wizard settings will also create and start a Mongrel server instance. The editor should be displaying the Aptana welcome screen shown in Figure 2-5. Open the Rails database configuration file at *config/database.yml* in the left Explorer window and edit the values for your database. You can start and stop your Mongrel server by navigating to the Servers tab found in the bottom center window. Select your Rails application in the list and use the controls to start the server in regular or debug mode.

Figure 2-5. RadRails Interface and Welcome screen

Discussion

The Rails Shell was introduced with RadRails version 1.0 and gives the developer access to Rails commands through a command-line interface. Choose the Console tab in the bottom panel or choose Open a Rails Shell in the console options. The shell and the location of the options button are shown in Figure 2-6. The Rails Shell complements the graphical interfaces for performing common Rails tasks and brings the IDE more in line with the Rails developers' preference of administering their application through a shell interface. The Rails Shell allows you to execute generator scripts, Rake tasks, and migrations, and create Rails projects and install gems and plugins.

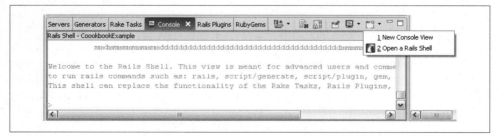

Figure 2-6. Aptana Rails Shell

See Also

- Recipe 1.11, "Setting Up Eclipse for JRuby Development"

2.20 Accessing Static Files in Your Rails Java EE Application

Problem

Warbler packages your Rails application by separating the static content from the executable code and moving it into the top-level directory in the WAR. This creates problems for some Rails functions such as `render :file` because the file paths it is generating are now incorrect. You would like your Rails application to serve static content in both a standard deployment and when assembled using Warbler.

Solution

Add a hook into your Rails application by creating a *public_dir.rb* file in the *initializers* directory. Evaluate the `$servlet_context` variable, which is only set when running in a Java EE environment, and set the location of the public directory based on the existence of the variable. Example 2-16 shows a technique for toggling the public directory.

Example 2-16. Public directory detection code

```
PUBLIC_DIR = if defined?($servlet_context)
    $servlet_context.getRealPath('/')
  else
    "#{RAILS_ROOT}" + '/public'
  end
```

Replace all the calls in your Rails code from `render :file => "/public/data/jobs.log"` to `render :file => "#{PUBLIC_DIR}/data/jobs.log"`.

Discussion

You will also need to patch Rails' internal functions that build paths to static files. The `render_optional_error_file` in `ActionController` can be patched by adding the code in Example 2-17 to your Rails *application.rb* file. A new module with patched method is mixed into the original `ActionController` module at runtime.

Example 2-17. Patching functions that serve static files

```
module Cookbook
 module PublicRescueExtensions
   protected
   def render_optional_error_file(status_code)
     status = interpret_status(status_code)
     path = "#{PUBLIC_DIR}/#{status[0,3]}.html"
     if File.exists?(path)
       render :file => path, :status => status
     else
       head status
     end
   end
 end
end
ActionController::Rescue.send :include,
  Cookbook::PublicRescueExtensions
```

See Also

• Recipe 2.2, "Packaging Rails As a Java EE Web Application"

## CHAPTER 3

Java Integration

3.0 Introduction

The first two chapters examined JRuby almost entirely from a Ruby-centric perspective. In the next few chapters, we look at leveraging JRuby more as a toolkit for Ruby and Java integration. There are two primary integration approaches that we will explore in this chapter. The first is how JRuby can be used to add functionality to a Java application; the second is how Ruby programs can take advantage of the wide array of preexisting Java libraries. Frequently, these types of integration are combined. For example, when mixing Java and Ruby code, using a consistent configuration for application logging can be useful, something which is explored in Recipe 3.4.

There are three primary APIs for embedding Ruby into a Java application:

- The JRuby low-level API
- The Bean Scripting Framework (BSF)
- Java Scripting, defined by JSR 223

These APIs are the subject of the first three recipes in this chapter. The differences between the low-level API and either BSF or Java Scripting are fairly obvious—the low-level API ties your Java code directly to JRuby, whereas both BSF and Java Scripting are abstractions of the JRuby runtime and, in fact, support multiple scripting languages. In general, you will use the JRuby API when you need tight control over the runtime's configuration. The choice between BSF and Java Scripting is largely based on deployment environment—BSF support is more consistent on Java 5, whereas Java Scripting is only available as a backport.

Regardless of the mechanics, the value of using JRuby in this way primarily stems from the fact that Ruby code is interpreted, not compiled. This allows you to store Ruby code in a Java `String` object and evaluate it while your application is running. For example, a reporting application could store the Ruby code necessary to generate a particular report in a database. Another scenario would be to have an application extensible through Ruby-based plugins that could be added or removed while the application is running, something not typically associated with Java applications. A similar technique has been used extensively in gaming, most notably the popular, massive multiplayer game World of Warcraft, which can be extended by users using the Lua scripting language (even though the core is written in C++).[*]

All of this power comes at a cost. The JRuby runtime, regardless of whether you use the low-level API, BSF, or Java Scripting, is expensive to create and operate. The creation expense relates to time: starting JRuby can take thousands of milliseconds. The operational expense relates to memory usage, most significantly in the permanent generation (PermGen) memory space. The former issue can be mitigated using a pool of runtimes, described in Recipe 3.8. The latter issue can usually be resolved by ensuring that enough PermGen space is available by using the -XX:PermSize command-line argument. Typically, a value of 256m is adequate. Recipe 2.7 has some additional discussion of memory issues with JRuby.

3.1 Executing Ruby from Java

Problem

You want to execute some Ruby code from a Java application.

Solution

Obtain an instance of org.jruby.Ruby and call the evalScriptlet() method. The org.jruby.javasupport.JavaEmbedUtils class provides static factory methods for creating an instance of the JRuby runtime. Example 3-1 shows a simple usage of these classes.

Example 3-1. Calling Ruby from Java

```
package org.jrubycookbook.ch03;

import java.util.Collections;

import org.jruby.Ruby;
import org.jruby.javasupport.JavaEmbedUtils;

public class RubyRunner {

    public static void main(String[] args) {
        // Create an instance of the JRuby runtime. The parameter to initalize()
        // is a list of paths to be added to the Ruby load path.
        Ruby runtime = JavaEmbedUtils.initialize(Collections.EMPTY_LIST);
        runtime.evalScriptlet("puts 'hello world'");
    }

}
```

---

[*] Obviously, great care must be taken when evaluating user-provided code in any environment.

When run, this class outputs the classic greeting:

```
hello world
```

 Prior to JRuby 1.0.3, the method used to obtain instances of the JRuby runtime was `Ruby.getDefaultInstance()`. Although this usage has been deprecated, you may see it from time to time in code examples.

Discussion

Every execution of `JavaEmbedUtils.initialize()` will create a new instance of the JRuby runtime. JRuby also provides a mechanism for reuse of JRuby runtimes within a single Java thread. To enable this, set the Java system property `jruby.runtime.threadlocal` to `"true"`. If this is set, calls to `JavaEmbedUtils.initialize()` will create a new instance and store that instance in a `ThreadLocal` variable. To access this instance, call `Ruby.get CurrentInstance()`. Example 3-2 illustrates instance reuse by setting and retrieving a global variable within the runtime.

Example 3-2. Using the current JRuby runtime

```java
package org.jrubycookbook.ch03;

import java.util.Collections;

import org.jruby.Ruby;
import org.jruby.javasupport.JavaEmbedUtils;

public class RubyRunner2 {

    public static void main(String[] args) {
        // Enable ThreadLocal support
        System.setProperty("jruby.runtime.threadlocal", "true");
        // Create a JRuby instance
        Ruby runtime = JavaEmbedUtils.initialize(Collections.EMPTY_LIST);
        // Execute a bit of Ruby code that creates a variable
        runtime.evalScriptlet("$message = 'hello world from JRuby'");
        runtime.evalScriptlet("$counter = 0");
        for (int i = 0; i < 5; i++) {
            outputMessage();
        }
    }

    private static void outputMessage() {
        Ruby runtime = Ruby.getCurrentInstance();
        String scriptlet = "puts \"<#{$counter}> #{$message}\"";
        runtime.evalScriptlet("$counter = $counter.next");
        runtime.evalScriptlet(scriptlet);
    }
}
```

When run, this class produces the following output:

```
<1> hello world from JRuby
<2> hello world from JRuby
<3> hello world from JRuby
<4> hello world from JRuby
<5> hello world from JRuby
```

Using the `Ruby` class, it is also possible to generate new instances of common JRuby classes and pass those instances to the JRuby runtime so that executed scripts can use them. The `main()` method from Example 3-2 could be rewritten using these methods like this:

```java
public static void main(String[] args) {
        System.setProperty("jruby.runtime.threadlocal", "true");
        Ruby runtime = getOrCreateInstance();
        RubyString message = runtime.newString("hello world");
        runtime.getGlobalVariables().set("$message", message);
        for (int i = 0; i < 5; i++) {
            outputMessage(i + 1);
        }
    }
}
```

JRuby runtimes have a load path based on the value of the `jruby.home` system property. The default load path elements for JRuby 1.1 are:

1. *jruby.home*/lib/ruby/site_ruby/1.8
2. *jruby.home*/lib/ruby/site_ruby
3. *jruby.home*/lib/ruby/1.8
4. *jruby.home*/lib/ruby/1.8/java
5. lib/ruby/1.8 (relative to the current working directory)
6. . (the current working directory)

When you use the *jruby* executable as described in Chapter 1, the `jruby.home` system property is set automatically based on the `JRUBY_HOME` environment variable. When writing Java applications that use JRuby, it's necessary to set this system property manually. You can set this system property using the `-D` command-line option:

```
java -cp bin:/opt/java/jruby-1.1/lib/jruby.jar\
-Djruby.home=/opt/java/jruby-1.1 org.jrubycookbook.ch03.RubyRunner
```

This system property can also be set by an IDE when running your application, such as the Eclipse Run... dialog seen in Figure 3-1, or a build script such as the Ant build script seen in Example 3-3.

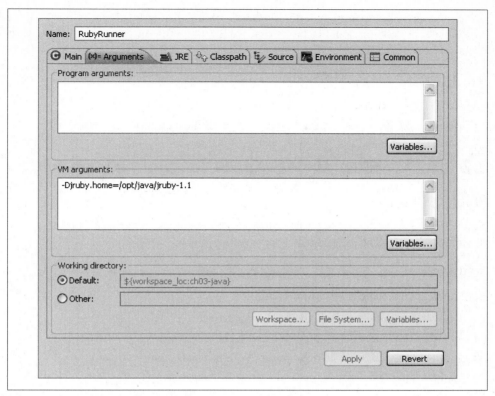

Figure 3-1. Setting the jruby.home system property with Eclipse

Example 3-3. Setting the jruby.home system property with Apache Ant

```xml
<?xml version="1.0" encoding="UTF-8"?>
<project name="project" default="run">
    <property name="jruby.home" value="/opt/java/jruby-1.1"/>

    <target name="run">
        <java classname="org.jrubycookbook.ch03.RubyRunner4" fork="true">
            <classpath>
                <pathelement location="bin"/>
                <pathelement location="${jruby.home}/lib/jruby.jar"/>
            </classpath>
            <sysproperty key="jruby.home" value="${jruby.home}"/>
        </java>
    </target>
</project>
```

If you have the `JRUBY_HOME` environment variable set, you may also be able to obtain this value by calling `System.getenv()` and using the value of the environment variable to set the `jruby.home` system property:

```
System.setProperty("jruby.home", System.getenv("JRUBY_HOME"));
```

As noted in the comments in Example 3-1, the `initialize()` method of `JavaEmbedUtils` accepts a list of paths that will be prepended to the default load path described earlier.

See Also

- Recipe 3.2, "Invoking JRuby Through the Bean Scripting Framework"
- Recipe 3.3, "Invoking JRuby Through Java Scripting Support"

3.2 Invoking JRuby Through the Bean Scripting Framework

Problem

You want to execute some Ruby code from a Java application and want the flexibility to support multiple scripting language implementations.

Solution

Use the Bean Scripting Framework (BSF):

1. Add *bsf.jar*, included with JRuby distributions, to your Java classpath.
2. Register the JRuby scripting engine with the BSF runtime.
3. Create an instance of the `org.apache.bsf.BSFManager` class.
4. Call the `eval()` or `exec()` method on the `BSFManager` object.

Example 3-4 shows a simple usage of JRuby through BSF.

Example 3-4. Invoking JRuby with BSF

```
package org.jrubycookbook.ch03;

import org.apache.bsf.BSFException;
import org.apache.bsf.BSFManager;

public class RubyBSFRunner {

    public static void main(String[] args) throws BSFException {
        BSFManager.registerScriptingEngine("ruby",
                "org.jruby.javasupport.bsf.JRubyEngine", new String[] { "rb" });
        BSFManager manager = new BSFManager();
        manager.exec("ruby", "<script>", 1, 1, "puts 'hello world'");
    }

}
```

Discussion

The Bean Scripting Framework is an open source software framework originally developed by IBM that is now part of the Apache Jakarta project. It provides a generic application programming interface (API) for supporting scripting languages within Java applications. BSF comes with built-in support for several scripting languages, including:

- JavaScript
- NetRexx
- Python
- Tcl
- XSLT

In addition to these languages, the Bean Scripting Framework defines a service provider interface (SPI) that allows other scripting languages to be plugged in by implementing the `org.apache.bsf.BSFEngine` interface. JRuby provides an implementation of this interface with the class `org.jruby.javasupport.bsf.JRubyEngine`. As you can see in Example 3-4, it is necessary to register this class with BSF by calling `BSFManager.register ScriptingEngine()`. When registering this engine implementation (or any other), you have to provide BSF with both the name of the scripting language (`ruby`) and a list of possible file extensions (`rb`). BSFManager provides two methods for invoking a scripting language: `eval()` and `exec()`. The difference between these two methods is that `eval()` is expected to return a value, whereas `exec()` is not. Both methods accept the name of the scripting engine to be invoked and some information used for error reporting and debugging: a source name (e.g., the filename when a script is loaded from a file), a line number, and a column number. Finally, the last parameter to both methods is the script content itself.

BSF provides a mechanism to expose Java objects to scripts. This is done using the `declareBean()` method of the `BSFManager` class. For JRuby, Java objects are made available as global variables within the JRuby runtime. Example 3-5 shows this functionality in use. Note that the variable name passed to `declareBean()` does not have the `$` prefix, while the reference to this variable from Ruby code does. The `$` prefix is automatically added to the variable name. This avoids adding Ruby-specific names into your code, thereby enabling you to more easily mix multiple scripting languages in the same application.

Example 3-5. Using declareBean()

```
package org.jrubycookbook.ch03;

import org.apache.bsf.BSFException;
import org.apache.bsf.BSFManager;

public class RubyBSFRunner2 {
```

```
public static void main(String[] args) throws BSFException {
    BSFManager.registerScriptingEngine("ruby",
            "org.jruby.javasupport.bsf.JRubyEngine", new String[] { "rb" });
    BSFManager manager = new BSFManager();
    manager.declareBean("message", "hello world", String.class);
    manager.exec("ruby", "<script>", 1, 1, "puts $message");
}

}
```

The BSF website, *http://jakarta.apache.org/bsf*, contains a variety of additional documentation about using BSF.

See Also

- Recipe 3.1, "Executing Ruby from Java"
- Recipe 3.3, "Invoking JRuby Through Java Scripting Support"

3.3 Invoking JRuby Through Java Scripting Support

Problem

You are running Java 6 (or later), and you want to execute some Ruby code from a Java application and want the flexibility to support multiple scripting language implementations.

Solution

Use Java's built-in scripting framework, defined in JSR (Java Specification Request) 223:

1. Download *jsr223-engines.zip* from *https://scripting.dev.java.net*.
2. Unzip the file *jruby/build/jruby-engine.jar* from *jsr223-engines.zip* and add it to your classpath.
3. Create an instance of `javax.script.ScriptEngineManager`.
4. Call `getEngineByName("ruby")` to obtain an instance of `javax.script.ScriptEngine`.
5. Call the `eval()` method on the `ScriptEngine` object.

Example 3-6 shows a simple usage of JRuby using the JSR 223 API.

Example 3-6. Invoking JRuby through javax.script.ScriptEngineManager

```
package org.jrubycookbook.ch03;

import javax.script.ScriptEngine;
import javax.script.ScriptEngineManager;
import javax.script.ScriptException;
```

```
public class Ruby223Runner {

    public static void main(String[] args) throws ScriptException {
        ScriptEngineManager scriptManager = new ScriptEngineManager();
        ScriptEngine engine = scriptManager.getEngineByName("ruby");
        engine.eval("puts 'hello world'");
    }

}
```

Discussion

JSR 223: Scripting for the Java Platform was one of the more highly anticipated upgrades to the Java platform in the Java 6 release. At the simplest level, it provides a standardized version of the API (and SPI) that the Bean Scripting Framework (BSF) had provided for many years. Almost more importantly, however, is the message that JSR 223 sends to the programming community as a whole by formalizing the distinction between Java the *language* and Java the *platform*. JSR 223's mere existence suggests that the Java platform will provide a suitable runtime environment for a variety of scripting languages, including Ruby/JRuby.

As you can see by comparing Example 3-6 with Example 3-4, the JSR 223 API is simpler to use than the BSF API in that proactive registration of scripting engines is not required. JSR 223 defines a discovery mechanism that allows script engines to be automatically discovered based on the existence of a file in the *META-INF* directory. When a script engine is discovered, the scripting runtime queries it for a number of attributes, including the file extensions typically associated with the engine and one or more names by which the script engine will be identified. In the case of JRuby, the script engine is registered with the names ruby and jruby and the file extension rb. Thus, any of these will return the JRuby engine:

```
scriptManager.getEngineByName("ruby");
scriptManager.getEngineByName("jruby");
scriptManager.getEngineByExtension("rb");
```

As with the native JRuby interface and BSF, the JSR 223 API provides a mechanism to pass Java objects into the scripting engine. In the case of JRuby, these objects become global variables in the JRuby runtime. Example 3-7 shows this functionality in action.

Example 3-7. Creating a global variable with JSR 223

```
package org.jrubycookbook.ch03;

import javax.script.ScriptEngine;
import javax.script.ScriptEngineManager;
import javax.script.ScriptException;

public class Ruby223Runner2 {

    public static void main(String[] args) throws ScriptException {
```

```
        ScriptEngineManager scriptManager = new ScriptEngineManager();
        ScriptEngine engine = scriptManager.getEngineByName("ruby");
        engine.put("message", "hello world");
        engine.eval("puts $message");
    }

}
```

As with BSF, the **$** variable prefix indicating a global Ruby variable is automatically prepended to the variable name.

Why Use BSF?

As you can see from these last two recipes, BSF and Java Scripting provide basically equivalent functionality. New applications are strongly advised to leverage the Java Scripting interface instead of BSF. That said, there are some reasons for using BSF instead of Java Scripting.

The most significant reason is Java 5 compatibility. A JAR file containing the core Java Scripting interfaces is available as a download for Java 5 environments from *http://jcp .org/aboutJava/communityprocess/final/jsr223/index.html*; the JRuby engine, however, requires Java 6.[†] So if you are running Java 5, using Java Scripting to interface with JRuby simply is not an option.

A secondary advantage to BSF is that the BSF JRuby engine is included with the JRuby distribution. This means that the BSF engine is guaranteed to work with the version of JRuby you are using. During the development cycle leading up to the release of JRuby 1.1, the native JRuby interface changed significantly several times and broke the existing Java Scripting engine.[‡]

Finally, for applications that use BSF already and are simply looking to add support for Ruby as an additional scripting language, continuing to use BSF is a logical course of action.

See Also

- Recipe 3.1, "Executing Ruby from Java"
- Recipe 3.2, "Invoking JRuby Through the Bean Scripting Framework"

[†] There is an open issue for this in the JSR223 engine project, *https://scripting.dev.java.net/issues/show_bug .cgi?id=28*.

[‡] In fact, at the time of writing, the JRuby engine in *jsr223-engines.zip* and *jsr223-engines.tar.gz* does not work with JRuby 1.1. A compatible engine (version 1.1.2) is available from *https://scripting.dev.java.net/ servlets/ProjectDocumentList?folderID=8848&expandFolder=8848&folderID=8847*.

3.4 Logging from Ruby with Jakarta Commons Logging

Problem

You are running Ruby code within a Java application that uses Jakarta Commons Logging (JCL) and wish your log messages to be consistent.

Solution

Use a class like the one in Example 3-8 to transform fully qualified Ruby class names into identifiers that resemble fully qualified Java class names.

Example 3-8. Custom JRuby LogFactory bridge class

```
package org.jrubycookbook.ch03;

import org.apache.commons.logging.Log;
import org.apache.commons.logging.LogFactory;

import org.jruby.RubyObject;

public class JRubyLogFactory {
    public static Log getLog(RubyObject o) {
        String rubyClassName = o.getMetaClass().getName();
        String logName = rubyClassName.replace("::", ".");
        return LogFactory.getLog(logName);
    }
}
```

Once this is in place, you can reference this class in your Ruby code and create new `Log` objects by passing `self` to the `getLog()` method. Log messages will be logged under a log name derived from the fully qualified Ruby class name. The script in Example 3-9 will log a message under the log name `Log.LogTest`.

Example 3-9. Using the JRubyLogFactory bridge class

```
include Java

import org.jrubycookbook.ch03.JRubyLogFactory

module Log
    class LogTest
        def initialize
            @log = JRubyLogFactory.getLog(self)
        end

        def hello
            @log.info("hello via jcl")
        end
    end
end

Log::LogTest.new.hello
```

Discussion

Jakarta Commons Logging is a popular Java library for providing a consistent logging API across several logging implementations, including Log4J, the `java.util.logging` package, LogKit, and JCL's own SimpleLog. JCL is especially popular amongst library developers as it allows the library to work with several logging implementations without having a compile-time dependency to any of them. Java code will typically obtain an implementation of the `org.apache.commons.logging.Log` interface by calling one of two factory methods:

- `LogFactory.getLog(Class)`
- `LogFactory.getLog(String)`

The former calls the latter passing the fully qualified class name. As many logging packages allow you to configure logging using a hierarchal model, i.e., all logs whose names begin with `org.apache.commons` log to a particular file, the class name has become a useful source of log names.

There are two reasons to write a bridge class such as that in Example 3-8. First, with JRuby, Ruby classes are *not* Java classes, so this code will fail:

```
@log = org.apache.commons.logging.LogFactory.getLog(self.class)
```

Second, although you could obtain the class name with code such as:

```
@log = org.apache.commons.logging.LogFactory.getLog(self.class.name)
```

The log name will have colons rather than the expected periods and logging implementations that were written with Java packages in mind will not recognize log names for classes in the same module as being related. Whether this will be a major issue depends upon how much logging your code is doing and how many individual classes you have.

You may have noticed that in Examples 3-8 and 3-9, the `getLog()` method accepts an instance of `org.jruby.RubyObject`. This could have been written to accept an instance of `org.jruby.RubyClass` and then referenced from Ruby code like this:

```
@log = JRubyLogFactory.getLog(self.class)
```

However, this is more verbose and has more potential to result in a variance in log names. The point of this exercise is to have consistent log names; encapsulating the logic for generating a log name from a Ruby object seems to make more sense. If you needed to have a nonstandard log name, you could always go back to the original `LogFactory.getLog()` method:

```
@log = org.apache.commons.logging.LogFactory.getLog("Some Other Log Name")
```

3.5 Using the Java Concurrency Utilities

Problem

You want to use the classes in the `java.util.concurrent` package to write code that is both thread-safe and highly performant.

Solution

Simply reference the classes in your Ruby code. For example, to create an instance of `java.util.concurrent.ConcurrentHashMap`, just use the constructor:

```
$hash = java.util.concurrent.ConcurrentHashMap.new
```

Likewise, the `java.util.concurrent.Executors` factory class can be used to create powerful yet easy-to-use thread pools. In Example 3-10, a thread pool containing two threads is created and used from Ruby code.

Example 3-10. Using a java.util.concurrent thread pool from Ruby

```ruby
include Java

class MyLongTask
    include java.util.concurrent.Callable

    def initialize(label)
        @label = label
    end

    def call
        puts "about to sleep in task labeled #{@label}\n"
        # artificially create a longer delay
        sleep 5
        puts "done sleeping in task labeled #{@label}\n"
        return "result of the long task labeled #{@label}\n"
    end
end

# create a new thread pool
executor = java.util.concurrent.Executors::newFixedThreadPool(2)

# create an array to store the future value references
future = Array.new

puts "submitting first task"
future[0] = executor.submit(MyLongTask.new("first"))

puts "submitting second task"
future[1] = executor.submit(MyLongTask.new("second"))

puts "submitting third task"
future[2] = executor.submit(MyLongTask.new("third"))
```

```
puts "All tasks have been submitted"

# this method call will block until the first task has completed
puts future[0].get()

# this method call will block until the second task has completed
puts future[1].get()

# this method call will block until the third task has completed
puts future[2].get()
```

The exact output of this code may vary slightly from execution to execution, but in general you will see all three tasks being submitted, followed by the first two tasks starting to sleep. Eventually, those tasks will complete and the third will start. However, since there are multiple threads, the first two tasks may be completed in any order, as seen here:

```
submitting first task
submitting second task
about to sleep in task labeled first
submitting third task
about to sleep in task labeled second
All tasks have been submitted
done sleeping in task labeled second
done sleeping in task labeled first
result of the long task labeled first
about to sleep in task labeled third
result of the long task labeled second
done sleeping in task labeled third
result of the long task labeled third
```

Discussion

When the JRuby runtime creates Ruby proxy objects for Java collection classes, it adds a variety of utility methods found in the corresponding Ruby collection class. This enables Java collection classes, including the concurrency-optimized classes in the `java.util.concurrent` packages to be treated like Ruby collections *in some, but not all, cases*. For example, when used from JRuby, `java.util.concurrent.ConcurrentHashMap` instances have an `each` method that behaves just like the `each` method from the Ruby `Hash` class, as seen in Example 3-11.

Example 3-11. Using a ConcurrentHashMap like a Hash

```
include Java
import java.util.concurrent.ConcurrentHashMap

states = ConcurrentHashMap.new
states['NY'] = 'New York'
states['ND'] = 'North Dakota'

states.each do |key,value|
    puts "The abbreviation for #{value} is #{key}."
end
```

Similar methods are added to instances of `java.util.List` and `java.util.Set`. However, you cannot use the Ruby `instance_of?` method to check if these objects are instances of the corresponding Ruby collection class. Instead, you can use the `respond_to?` method to check the availability of individual methods:

```
irb(main):001:0> java.util.concurrent.CopyOnWriteArrayList.new.respond_to? 'each'
=> true
```

3.6 Creating JavaBean Style Accessor Methods

Problem

Ruby developers use the `attr_accessor` function as a convenient way to declare instance variables and create `read` and `write` methods in a class. You would like a similar function that can add JavaBean-style `get` and `set` methods to a class with a condensed and declarative syntax.

Solution

Start by creating a Ruby module that will contain the new method. The function can be coded directly into your classes, but the module encourages more reusable and less repetitive code. Create a method called `java_attr_accessor` that accepts a list of symbols, consistent with Ruby's `attr_accessor` method. The symbols are named with the Ruby style of using underscores as word delimiters, but the function will convert each symbol into the JavaBean-style equivalent name by adding the `get` and `set` prefixes to the camel case representation of the name. Example 3-12 shows the module and a class that adds several instance variables using the `java_attr_accessor` method after extending the new module.

Example 3-12. Helper module for JavaBean accessors

```
module Helper
  def java_attr_accessor(*symbols)
    symbols.each { |symbol|
      camelcased = symbol.to_s.capitalize.gsub(/\_[a-zA-Z]/) {|s| s[1..1].upcase}
      module_eval( "def get#{camelcased}() @#{symbol}; end" )
      module_eval( "def set#{camelcased}(val) @#{symbol} = val; end" )
    }
  end
end

class Example
      extend Helper
      java_attr_accessor :title,:first_name
end

mc = Example.new
mc.setTitle('Cookbook')
mc.setFirstName("John")
```

Discussion

This utility function can be very useful when working with applications or frameworks that make heavy use of JavaBeans, such as Hibernate and Spring.

3.7 Writing Consistent Code

Problem

You are calling both Ruby and Java libraries from Ruby and want the code to look consistent. This line from Example 3-9 is very obviously calling a Java method:

```
@log = JRubyLogFactory.getLog(self)
```

Solution

Replace camel-cased method names with method names that follow the Ruby naming convention: all lowercase letters and underscores for word separators. The line from Example 3-9 referenced above could be rewritten as:

```
@log = JRubyLogFactory.get_log(self)
```

JRuby provides this automatic method translation as a way of blending Java and Ruby method calls together.

Discussion

JRuby won't override an existing method. If there was an actual method named `get_log()`, it takes precedence. That caveat aside, using this feature leads to a more consistent coding style.

3.8 Transforming XML with TrAX

Problem

You want to transform XML documents using XSLT through Java's Transformation API for XML (TrAX).

Solution

Import the class `javax.xml.transform.TransformerFactory` as well as the classes to be used for the input and output, typically `javax.xml.transform.stream.StreamSource` and `javax.xml.transform.stream.StreamResult`. If you will be transforming with the same stylesheet repeatedly, create a `javax.xml.transform.Templates` object to save the compiled stylesheet. If this is a one-time transformation, simply create a `javax.xml.transform.Transformer` object. Example 3-13 shows both scenarios.

Example 3-13. Using TrAX from JRuby

```
include Java

import javax.xml.transform.TransformerFactory
import javax.xml.transform.stream.StreamResult
import javax.xml.transform.stream.StreamSource

# Create a new TransformerFactory instance
factory = TransformerFactory.new_instance

# Compile a stylesheet into a Template object
style_input = StreamSource.new("rss.xslt")
templates = factory.new_templates(style_input)

# Setup sources for input and output
input = StreamSource.new("http://www.mtv.com/rss/news/news_full.jhtml")
output = StreamResult.new(java.lang.System.out)

# Create a new Transformer from the Template object
transformer = templates.new_transformer

# Do the transformation
transformer.transform(input, output)

# Simplified - just create a new Transformer from the stylesheet
transformer = factory.new_transformer(style_input)
transformer.transform(input, output)
```

Discussion

TrAX includes a few interfaces that can be easily implemented in Ruby to customize the transformation process. The interface `javax.xml.transform.ErrorListener` receives callbacks from the `Transformer` object whenever a warning or error is encountered. Example 3-14 shows a simple implementation of this interface in Ruby.

Example 3-14. Implementing javax.xml.transform.ErrorListener in Ruby

```
class ErrorCounter
  attr_reader :errors
  attr_reader :warnings
  attr_reader :fatals

  def error(ex)
    @errors = 0 if (@errors == nil)
    @errors = @errors + 1
  end

  def warning(ex)
    @warnings = 0 if (@warnings == nil)
    @warnings = @warnings + 1
  end

  def fatalError(ex)
    @fatals = 0 if (@fatals == nil)
```

```
    @fatals = @fatals + 1
  end
end

# Use the ErrorCounter class
counter = ErrorCounter.new
transformer = factory.new_transformer(style_input)
transformer.error_listener = counter
transformer.transform(input, output)

p "Errors: #{counter.errors}"
```

Another TrAX interface of note is `javax.xml.transform.URIResolver`, which allows you to intercept references made from a stylesheet to external resources. The `URIResolver` implementation in Example 3-15 shows a simple usage of this interface to intercept a relative reference for a stylesheet. This interception was done whether *rss.xslt* was referenced using the XSLT `document()` function, `xsl:import`, or `xsl:include`. For any other URI, the `resolve` method will return `nil`, meaning that the `Transformer` should resolve the URI itself.

Example 3-15. Implementing javax.xml.transform.URIResolver in Ruby

```
class MySiteResolver
  def resolve(href,base)
    if (href == 'rss.xslt')
      return StreamSource.new('http://www.mysite.com/rss.xslt')
    end
  end
end
```

3.9 Creating a Pool of JRuby Runtimes

Problem

You need to execute Ruby code that is not thread-safe and requires exclusive control of the JRuby runtime and do not want to create new runtimes per thread.

Solution

Use the Jakarta Commons Pool library to create a pool of JRuby runtimes. When your code needs to invoke JRuby, borrow a runtime from the pool and return it when finished. To start, download Jakarta Commons Pool from *http://jakarta.apache.org/commons/pool/* and add the JAR file to your classpath. Create a subclass of `org.apache.commons.pool.BasePoolableObjectFactory` that creates JRuby runtimes using the methods described in Recipe 3.1. Then use this factory object to construct an `org.apache.commons.pool.impl.GenericObjectPool`. Example 3-16 shows a subclass of `GenericObjectPool` built for pooling JRuby runtimes.

Example 3-16. Creating a pool of JRuby runtimes

```
package org.jrubycookbook.ch03;

import java.util.Collections;
import java.util.Date;

import org.apache.commons.pool.BasePoolableObjectFactory;
import org.apache.commons.pool.impl.GenericObjectPool;
import org.jruby.Ruby;
import org.jruby.javasupport.JavaEmbedUtils;

public class JRubyRuntimePool extends GenericObjectPool {

    private static class JRubyRuntimeFactory extends BasePoolableObjectFactory {

        public Object makeObject() throws Exception {
            Ruby runtime = JavaEmbedUtils.initialize(Collections.EMPTY_LIST);
            return runtime;
        }

    }

    public JRubyRuntimePool() {
        super(new JRubyRuntimeFactory());
    }

    public Ruby borrowRuntime() throws Exception {
        return (Ruby) borrowObject();
    }

    public void returnRuntime(Ruby runtime) throws Exception {
        returnObject(runtime);
    }

    public static void main(String[] args) throws Exception {
        JRubyRuntimePool pool = new JRubyRuntimePool();
        // always have a minimum of five runtimes available in the pool.
        pool.setMinIdle(5);

        // if there are more than 10 runtimes in the pool, remove the extras
        pool.setMaxIdle(10);

        // and don't allow more than 40 runtimes to be in use at the same time
        pool.setMaxActive(40);

        // check every minute that the minimum and maximum idle counts are met
        pool.setTimeBetweenEvictionRunsMillis(60000);

        // start the application
    }
}
```

Discussion

The `GenericObjectPool` class has a variety of configuration parameters, including:

maxActive

> The maximum number of objects that can be borrowed from the pool at one time. Can be unlimited. The default is 8.

maxIdle

> The maximum number of objects that can sit idle in the pool at any time. Can be unlimited. The default is 8.

minIdle

> The minimum number of objects that will be idle in the pool. If the pool drops below this threshold (and `timeBetweenEvictionRunsMills` is greater than zero, see below), new instances will be created. The default is 0.

whenExhaustedAction

> Specifies the behavior of the pool when the pool is empty and a request to borrow an object is received. Can be to `fail` (throw a `java.util.NoSuchElementExcep tion`), `grow`, or to `block`. Defaults to `block`.

timeBetweenEvictionRunsMills

> Defines the time delay between runs of an asynchronous task that enforces that the `maxIdle` and `minIdle` properties. By default, this task is disabled.

Because the JRuby runtime is time-consuming to create, be sure to use the `minIdle` and the `timeBetweenEvictionRunsMills` properties.

See Also

- The Jakarta Commons Pool website, *http://commons.apache.org/pool/*
- *http://jruby-extras.rubyforge.org/svn/trunk/rails-integration/*, GoldSpike source code

3.10 Performing Remote Management with JMX

Problem

You want to write a client using Java Management Extensions (JMX) in Ruby to manage a remote Java application.

Solution

Use the `jmx4r` Ruby gem. This library significantly simplifies use of the JMX API. To install `jmx4r`:

```
jruby -S gem install jmx4r
```

To establish a connection with a JMX service, use the **establish_connection** class method:

```
JMX::MBean.establish_connection :host => "localhost", :port => 1099
```

To find an MBean by name, use the `find_by_name` class method:

```
os = JMX::MBean.find_by_name "java.lang:type=OperatingSystem"
```

The `find_by_name` method returns a dynamic object based around the MBean interface. In the case of the MBean named `java.lang:type=OperatingSystem`, the Java Virtual Machine exposes an MBean with several attributes about the underlying operating system. These JMX attributes can be simply accessed as properties. For example, to output the number of available processors:

```
p "Running with #{os.available_processors} processors."
```

 The actual attribute name is `AvailableProcessors`. The jmx4r library converts this name into a more Ruby-like form.

Similarly, JMX operations are invoked as method calls. For example, to force a garbage collection:

```
memory = JMX::MBean.find_by_name "java.lang:type=Memory"
memory.gc
```

Discussion

The jmx4r library also supports the ability to query for MBeans. Example 3-17 shows this functionality in action. In this example, JMX is used to discover the available JMS queues in an Apache ActiveMQ JMS server.

Example 3-17. Querying MBeans

```
include Java

require 'rubygems'
gem 'jmx4r'
require 'jmx4r'

JMX::MBean.establish_connection :host => "localhost", :port => 1099

queues = JMX::MBean.find_all_by_name \
    "org.apache.activemq:BrokerName=localhost,Type=Queue,*"

queues.each do |queue|
    p "Queue #{queue.name} contains #{queue.queue_size} queued messages."
end
```

Depending on the available queues, the output might be similar to this:

```
Queue LogQueue contains 25 queued messages.
Queue OrderQueue contains 5 queued messages.
```

See Also

- jmx4r website, *http://code.google.com/p/jmx4r/*
- *Java Management Extensions* by J. Steven Perry (O'Reilly)

3.11 Accessing Native Libraries with JRuby

Problem

You want to access native libraries such as Windows DLLs or Unix shared objects (.so) from JRuby.

Solution

Use the Java Native Access (JNA) API to access the operating system's libraries using only Java or any other JVM-based language like JRuby. JNA uses a dynamic architecture that eliminates the chore of creating, compiling, and distributing native interface files, which was required in other Java frameworks like the Java Native Interface (JNI). Example 3-18 shows how you can access the disk information from calls to the native Windows libraries.

Example 3-18. JNA example showing Windows disk space

```
include Java

import com.sun.jna.ptr.LongByReference

Kernel32 = com.sun.jna.NativeLibrary.getInstance('kernel32')
GetDiskFreeSpace = Kernel32.getFunction('GetDiskFreeSpaceExA')
avail = LongByReference.new
total = LongByReference.new
total_free = LongByReference.new
num = GetDiskFreeSpace.invokeInt(["C:\\", avail, total, total_free].to_java)
puts "available: #{avail.value}"
puts "total: #{total.value}"
puts "total_free #{total_free.value}"
```

Discussion

JNA is a great match with JRuby and makes it easier to create cross-platform applications that run inside the Java Virtual Machine while still accessing platform-specific APIs. The dynamic architecture is also philosophically in tune with Ruby development because it uses designs that eliminate extraneous code and facilitates rapid development.

See Also

- Java Native Access website, *https://jna.dev.java.net*

## CHAPTER 4

Enterprise Java

4.0 Introduction

As discussed in the introduction to Chapter 1, one of JRuby's great strengths is its ability to seamlessly interact with the wide variety of available Java libraries. One of the areas where this is most relevant is in the so-called enterprise domain, where Java has become well entrenched. Much of Java's success has come from the Java Enterprise Edition (Java EE, formerly known as J2EE) platform standards. But platforms that are not Java standards have been just as critical. Two will be covered in this chapter: Spring Framework and Hibernate.[*] Regardless of whether a particular technology is a standard or not, all enterprise Java platforms are designed to enable developers to focus on developing business and presentation logic rather than infrastructure and integration.

This chapter starts with a recipe about using Java Naming and Directory Interface (JNDI) objects from Ruby. As its name implies, JNDI is an API for accessing directory services. JNDI presents application developers with a unified interface that can span various services and service types. Within a Java EE application server, JNDI is used by application code to discover resources managed by the server. These could be data sources (a subject discussed throughout Chapter 2), Enterprise JavaBeans (EJBs), Java Messaging Service (JMS) objects, and a variety of other resources. Your Java EE application server documentation should provide complete details on what resources are available and how you can add additional resources to the server. JNDI can also be used to access external services. In the second and third recipes, we use JNDI to connect to a remote JMS broker using the Apache ActiveMQ server so that we can send and receive JMS messages. In a later recipe, we use JNDI to connect to a Lightweight Directory Access Protocol (LDAP) server and use JRuby to simplify the JNDI API.

Following JMS, we will look at implementing an Enterprise JavaBean (EJB). Thanks to the support for annotation-based configuration that arrived with EJB 3, EJB development has become much simpler, yet the lack of annotation support in JRuby means

---

[*] For some time, the combination of Spring and Hibernate was being referred to as J3EE, but this term seems to have disappeared in recent years.

that you still have to write a small amount of bridge code to implement EJBs. Although JRuby and EJB may seem like an odd match at first, the EJB model can provide some significant benefits when being used with JRuby because of the instance pooling provided by Java EE containers. These containers all perform instance pooling for EJBs and only allow one consumer per EJB instance at a time. This means that when writing an EJB, whether using Java or Ruby, you do not need to worry about concurrency: the container does it for you. Many Ruby libraries, most notably ActiveRecord and Rails, have known concurrency problems; using EJBs eliminates the need to create custom instance pools as described in Recipe 3.9 and in the discussion of Rails in Chapter 2.

There are several recipes in this chapter that discuss JRuby integration with the Spring Framework, sometimes referred to as just Spring. Spring is, at the core, a platform for creating applications by defining application components (in the form of Java classes) and the relationships between them. This is known as Dependency Injection (DI) and/or Inversion of Control (IoC).[†] Leveraging this core platform, Spring also provides support for Aspect-Orientated Programming (AOP), transactions, authentication and authorization, remoting, model-view-controller (MVC) web development, and much more. Since version 2.0, Spring has provided support for dynamic languages, including JRuby. This support, the focus of several recipes, allows for objects defined in JRuby to be transparently integrated with objects defined in Java (or other dynamic languages).

This chapter also covers the Object-Relational Mapping (ORM) framework Hibernate as well as the Java Persistence API (JPA).[‡] Due to JRuby's Java integration, using these frameworks from JRuby isn't terribly complicated; mostly Hibernate and JPA just work. As a result, the recipes are about using JRuby as a productivity booster for these APIs.

4.1 Creating a JNDI Context

Problem

You need to create a JNDI `Context` object in order to connect to an LDAP server or JMS broker.

Solution

Create a Ruby hash with the properties you want to use as the environment and then pass this hash to the constructor of `javax.naming.InitialContext`, wrapping it in a

---

[†] Strictly speaking, Dependency Injection is a particular application of the Inversion of Control pattern, but in practice the terms are frequently used interchangeably.

[‡] Which is, in many ways, a standardized version of Hibernate.

`java.util.Hashtable` object. For example, the code in Example 4-1 creates a JNDI Context using the University of Michigan's public LDAP server.

Example 4-1. Creating a custom JNDI Context

```
include Java

import java.util.Hashtable
import javax.naming.InitialContext
import javax.naming.Context

env = {Context::INITIAL_CONTEXT_FACTORY => "com.sun.jndi.ldap.LdapCtxFactory",
       Context::PROVIDER_URL => "ldap://ldap.itd.umich.edu:389" }

ctx = InitialContext.new(Hashtable.new(env))
```

Discussion

Although JRuby will coerce Ruby hashes into Java objects that implement the `java.util.Map` interface, `InitialContext` objects are configured using a `Hashtable`. As a result, the hash must be wrapped by a `Hashtable`.

The properties used to instantiate the `InitialContext` object can also be stored in a file called *jndi.properties* in the Java classpath. In the case of Example 4-1, the following would be the contents of *jndi.properties*:

```
java.naming.factory.initial = com.sun.jndi.ldap.LdapCtxFactory
java.naming.provider.url = ldap://ldap.itd.umich.edu:389
```

With this configuration in place, the `InitialContext` can be easily created using the no-argument constructor:

```
ctx = InitialContext.new
```

Regardless of how it is configured, the value of the `java.naming.factory.initial` property must be a class available on the classpath. As discussed in Recipe 1.7, JRuby has the ability to add JAR files to the classpath dynamically. However, that capability does not apply to classes used in this type of factory class. This is because JAR files added dynamically to the classpath by JRuby are only visible from Ruby code. Throughout the next recipe, for example, the `java.naming.factory.initial` property is set to `org.apache.activemq.jndi.ActiveMQInitialContextFactory`. If you tried to add this class (and its dependencies) to the classpath in JRuby, a `javax.naming.NoInitial ContextException` will be thrown:

```
$ jirb
irb(main):001:0> include Java
irb(main):002:0>
irb(main):003:0* require '/opt/java/libs/geronimo-j2ee-management_1.0_spec-1.0.jar'
irb(main):004:0> require '/opt/java/libs/geronimo-jms_1.1_spec-1.1.1.jar'
irb(main):005:0> require '/opt/java/libs/activemq-core-5.1.0.jar'
irb(main):006:0>
irb(main):007:0* import java.util.Hashtable
irb(main):008:0> import javax.naming.InitialContext
```

```
irb(main):009:0> import javax.naming.Context
irb(main):010:0>
irb(main):011:0* env = { Context::INITIAL_CONTEXT_FACTORY =>
irb(main):012:1*          "org.apache.activemq.jndi.ActiveMQInitialContextFactory",
irb(main):013:1*          Context::PROVIDER_URL =>
irb(main):014:1*          "tcp://localhost:61616" }
irb(main):015:0> ctx = InitialContext.new(Hashtable.new(env))
NativeException: javax.naming.NoInitialContextException: Cannot instantiate class:\
     org.apache.activemq.jndi.ActiveMQInitialContextFactory
```

There is a solution to the problem—instantiate the class directly:

```
import org.apache.activemq.jndi.ActiveMQInitialContextFactory

env = { Context::PROVIDER_URL => "tcp://localhost:61616" }
ctx = ActiveMQInitialContextFactory.new.get_initial_context(Hashtable.new(env))
```

See Also

- The JNDI website, *http://java.sun.com/products/jndi/*

4.2 Sending JMS Messages

Problem

Your application needs to send messages to a Java Messaging Service (JMS) message broker.

Solution

Add any necessary JAR files to the classpath. Create a `javax.naming.InitialContext` object as described in Recipe 4.1. The environment settings will be documented by the JMS broker vendor. For example, to connect to an instance of Apache ActiveMQ, you would use these properties:

```
env = { Context::INITIAL_CONTEXT_FACTORY =>
        "org.apache.activemq.jndi.ActiveMQInitialContextFactory",
        Context::PROVIDER_URL =>
        "tcp://localhost:61616" }
```

Once the `InitialContext` has been properly created, look up the JMS `Connection Factory` and `Destination` objects:

```
connection_factory = ctx.lookup("ConnectionFactory")
destination = ctx.lookup("dynamicQueues/output.queue")
```

The rest is simply JMS boilerplate, which we can encapsulate into a Ruby class as seen in Example 4-2.

Example 4-2. Sending a JMS message from Ruby

```
include Java

import java.util.Hashtable
import javax.naming.InitialContext
import javax.naming.Context
import javax.jms.Session

class JmsSender

  def initialize(environment)
    @context = InitialContext.new(Hashtable.new(environment))
    @connection_factory = @context.lookup("ConnectionFactory")
  end

  def send_text_message(destination_name, message_text)
    destination = @context.lookup(destination_name)
    connection = @connection_factory.create_connection()
    session = connection.create_session(false, Session::AUTO_ACKNOWLEDGE)
    producer = session.create_producer(destination)
    message = session.create_text_message
    message.text = message_text
    producer.send(message)
    session.close
  end
end

env = { Context::INITIAL_CONTEXT_FACTORY =>
        "org.apache.activemq.jndi.ActiveMQInitialContextFactory",
        Context::PROVIDER_URL =>
        "tcp://localhost:61616" }
sender = JmsSender.new(env)

sender.send_text_message("dynamicQueues/output.queue", "hello to JMS from Ruby")
```

This message can then be seen in the ActiveMQ administrative web client, as in Figure 4-1.

Discussion

As discussed in Recipe 4.1, to create a `javax.naming.InitialContext` object using `org.apache.activemq.jndi.ActiveMQInitialContextFactory`, the ActiveMQ JAR files must be on the classpath when the application starts—not added dynamically by JRuby.

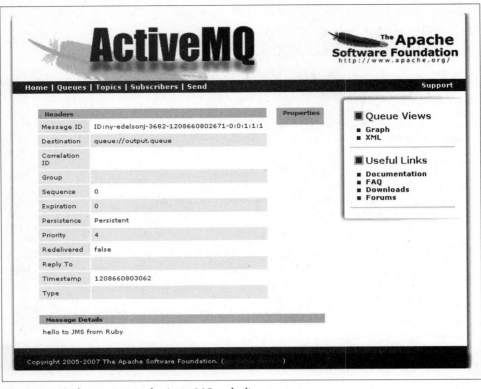

Figure 4-1. JRuby message in the ActiveMQ web client

The JMS API defines five different types of messages:

Stream
> Defined by the `javax.jms.StreamMessage` interface, messages of this type contain one or more Java primitives or objects in sequential order.

Map
> Defined by the `javax.jms.MapMessage` interface, messages of this type contain one or more name-value pairs. The names are Java `String` objects and the values can be primitives or objects.

Text
> Defined by the `javax.jms.TextMessage` interface, messages of this type contain a single `String` object.

Object
> Defined by the `javax.jms.ObjectMessage` interface, these messages contain a Java object that implements the `Serializable` interface.

Bytes

Defined by the `javax.jms.BytesMessage` interface, this message type is largely to support existing (i.e., non-JMS) messaging systems.

All of these message types can be used from JRuby, but special care must be taken when sending objects as JRuby objects are not correctly handled using Java serialization. This is true even if the message receiver is a JRuby application. For example, let's add a `send_object_message` method to the class from Example 4-2:

```
def send_object_message(destination_name, message_object)
  destination = @context.lookup(destination_name)
  connection = @connection_factory.create_connection()
  session = connection.create_session(false, Session::AUTO_ACKNOWLEDGE)
  producer = session.create_producer(destination)
  message = session.create_object_message message_object
  producer.send(message)
  session.close
end
```

If you were to call this message with a Ruby array:

```
arr = ["one", "two", "three"]
send_object_message("dynamicQueues/output.queue, arr)
```

An exception would be thrown when this message was received because the array is serialized as an `org.jruby.RubyArray` object. Instead, you should create a `java.util.ArrayList` object from this Ruby array:

```
arr = ["one", "two", "three"]
send_object_message("dynamicQueues/output.queue, java.util.ArrayList.new(arr))
```

4.3 Receiving JMS Messages

Problem

Your application needs to receive messages from a JMS message broker.

Solution

The initial setup is similar to sending JMS messages: create a JNDI `InitialContext` object and look up the `ConnectionFactory` and destination from the JNDI context. Using the `ConnectionFactory`, create a `Connection` object and from the `Connection`, create a `Session` object. The `Session` object can be used to create a `MessageConsumer` for a destination. The `MessageConsumer` object has two methods for receiving messages, both named `receive`. If `receive` is called with no arguments, then the method blocks until a message is available. If `receive` is called with an argument (which must be numeric), the method blocks until a message is available or the specific number of milliseconds passes.

Example 4-3 contains some basic code for receiving a message. Once the message is received, it is inspected to see if it is a text message and, if so, the text is output.

Example 4-3. Receiving a JMS message

```
include Java

import java.util.Hashtable
import javax.naming.InitialContext
import javax.naming.Context
import javax.jms.Session

env = { Context::INITIAL_CONTEXT_FACTORY =>
        "org.apache.activemq.jndi.ActiveMQInitialContextFactory",
        Context::PROVIDER_URL =>
        "tcp://localhost:61616" }

context = InitialContext.new(Hashtable.new(env))
connection_factory = context.lookup("ConnectionFactory")

destination = context.lookup("dynamicQueues/output.queue")
connection = connection_factory.create_connection()
session = connection.create_session(false, Session::AUTO_ACKNOWLEDGE)
consumer = session.create_consumer(destination)

connection.start

message = consumer.receive
if (message.respond_to? 'text')
 p "message = #{message.text}"
else
 p "message isn't a text message"
end

connection.stop
session.close
```

Discussion

Note that in Example 4-3, we start the connection before receiving a message. A running connection is required before receiving messages whereas it is not for sending messages.

4.4 Implementing an Enterprise JavaBean with JRuby

Problem

You want to encapsulate some Ruby code into an Enterprise JavaBean (EJB) in order to easily integrate it with other EJBs and servlets as well as take advantage of EJB container-provided services such as instance pooling, security, and transactions.

Solution

Create an interface and implementation class for your EJB. A simple EJB interface, annotated with `@Local` is in Example 4-4.

Example 4-4. EJB local interface

```
package org.jrubycookbook.j2ee.ejb;

import javax.ejb.Local;

@Local
public interface Reverser {
    public String reverse(String string);
}
```

In the implementation class, create an initialization method and use it to create an instance of the JRuby runtime. This could be done with any of the techniques discussed in Chapter 3. Annotate this initialization method with the `@PostConstruct` annotation. Then in each business method (i.e., those defined by the EJB interface), wrap the method arguments in Ruby objects, add them to the runtime, and finally execute the appropriate block of Ruby code. Example 4-5 includes a JRuby-based EJB class. In this example, the code is inline, but it could just as easily be in an external file.

Example 4-5. JRuby EJB

```
package org.jrubycookbook.j2ee.ejb;

import javax.annotation.PostConstruct;
import javax.ejb.Stateless;

import org.jruby.Ruby;
import org.jruby.RubyString;
import org.jruby.javasupport.JavaEmbedUtils;

@Stateless
public class ReverserBean implements Reverser {

    private Ruby ruby;

    @PostConstruct
    public void init() {
        ruby = JavaEmbedUtils.initialize(Collections.EMPTY_LIST);
    }

    public String reverse(String string) {
        ruby.getGlobalVariables().set("$message", ruby.newString(string));
        return ruby.evalScriptlet("$message.reverse").asJavaString();
    }

}
```

This EJB can then be accessed by servlets and other EJBs in the same container. Example 4-6 includes a servlet that uses this EJB.

Example 4-6. Servlet accessing the JRuby EJB

```
package org.jrubycookbook.j2ee.servlet;

import java.io.IOException;

import javax.ejb.EJB;
import javax.servlet.ServletException;
import javax.servlet.http.HttpServlet;
import javax.servlet.http.HttpServletRequest;
import javax.servlet.http.HttpServletResponse;

import org.jrubycookbook.j2ee.ejb.Reverser;

public class ReverseServlet extends HttpServlet {

    @EJB
    private Reverser reverser;

    protected void doGet(HttpServletRequest req, HttpServletResponse resp)
            throws ServletException, IOException {
        String result = reverser.reverse(req.getParameter("word"));
        resp.getWriter().println(result);
    }

}
```

A remote interface could also be defined and annotated with **@Remote**, which would make this EJB accessible remotely using Remote Method Invocation (RMI).

Discussion

As you can see, the class in Example 4-5 is just a bridge between the EJB container and the JRuby runtime. In large part, this is necessary because JRuby does not yet support Java annotations. If annotation support is added to JRuby in the future, it may be possible to eliminate the class (and perhaps the interface as well). It seems also likely that Java EE container vendors will add direct support for JRuby-based EJBs if there is demand for it.

The class in Example 4-5 is a stateless session bean (SLSB), but this same technique would hold true for stateful session beans (SFSBs) and message-driven beans (MDBs). You can also easily expose this EJB through a web service interface by adding some additional annotations, seen in Example 4-7.

Example 4-7. JRuby EJB with web service annotations

```
package org.jrubycookbook.j2ee.ejb;

import javax.jws.WebMethod;
import javax.jws.WebService;
```

```
// Other imports from Recipe 4-5

@WebService(targetNamespace = "http://jrubycookbook.org/ejb")
@Stateless
public class ReverserBean implements Reverser {

    private Ruby ruby;

// init() method from Example 4-5

    @WebMethod
    public String reverse(String string) {
        RubyString message = ruby.newString(string);
        ruby.getGlobalVariables().set("$message", message);
        return ruby.evalScriptlet("$message.reverse").asJavaString();
    }

}
```

Figure 4-2 shows this web service being tested through the web service testing interface included with the Sun Java System Application Server.

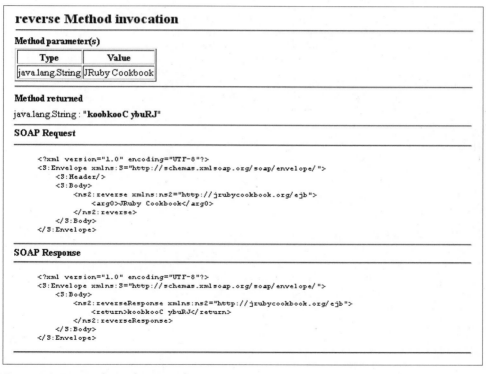

Figure 4-2. Testing the JRuby EJB web service

See Also

- Recipe 3.9, "Creating a Pool of JRuby Runtimes"

4.5 Defining Spring Beans in JRuby

Problem

You use the Spring Framework as a Dependency Injection (DI) container and wish to define some of your beans with JRuby.

Solution

Create a Java interface that defines the methods you will be implementing in your Ruby class. Use `jruby` element within the `lang` namespace in the Spring XML configuration to define a bean using both the interface and the location of the Ruby script. JRuby beans can also be configured using the `lang:property` element. A simple JRuby bean definition can be seen in Example 4-8.

Example 4-8. Simple Spring JRuby bean definition

```
1 <?xml version="1.0" encoding="UTF-8"?>
2 <beans xmlns="http://www.springframework.org/schema/beans"
3     xmlns:xsi="http://www.w3.org/2001/XMLSchema-instance"
4     xmlns:lang="http://www.springframework.org/schema/lang"
5     xsi:schemaLocation="http://www.springframework.org/schema/beans
6         http://www.springframework.org/schema/beans/spring-beans.xsd
7         http://www.springframework.org/schema/lang
8         http://www.springframework.org/schema/lang/spring-lang.xsd">
9
10    <lang:jruby id="rubyListener"
11        script-interfaces="org.jrubycookbook.ch04.Listener"
12        script-source="classpath:org/jrubycookbook/ch04/ruby_listener.rb">
13        <lang:property name="prefix" value="(from Ruby) " />
14    </lang:jruby>
15
16 </beans>
```

In this example, lines 2 through 8 are the boilerplate Spring configuration needed to set up both the default and `lang` namespaces. Lines 10 through 14 contain the actual bean definition including the setting of a property named `prefix`. The interface is defined in Example 4-9 and the Ruby implementation is in Example 4-10.

Example 4-9. Simple interface for Spring bean

```
package org.jrubycookbook.ch04;

public interface Listener {
    public void receiveMessage(String message);
}
```

Example 4-10. Ruby script referenced from Spring configuration

```
class RubyListener
    # setter for prefix property
    def setPrefix(p)
        @prefix = p
    end

    # implementation of Listener interface
    def receiveMessage(s)
        puts "#{@prefix}Got Message: #{s}"
    end
end

RubyListener.new
```

Note that for Spring to set the `prefix` property, a `setPrefix()` method must be defined. If we were writing traditional Ruby code, this method would likely be called `prefix=` and you would have generated the method with `attr_accessor` or `attr_writer`. But because Spring is based on the JavaBean standard, it expects a method named `setPrefix()`.

To use JRuby with Spring, your classpath must include the following JAR files, all of which are included in the Spring distribution:§

- *spring.jar*
- *asm-2.2.3.jar*
- *backport-util-concurrent.jar*
- *cglib-nodep-2.1_3.jar*
- *commons-logging.jar*
- *jruby.jar*

 At the time of writing, Spring's support for JRuby was not compatible with the 1.1; only JRuby 1.0 is supported.

Discussion

Spring's dynamic language support, which currently also includes support for Groovy and BeanShell in addition to JRuby, works by creating a dynamic proxy object that implements the interfaces listed in the `script-interfaces` attribute. This proxy receives the actual method calls and delegates to the object created by the script file referenced in the `script-source` attribute. The syntax of the script-source attribute is the standard Spring syntax for accessing resources. In Example 4-8, we are referencing a Ruby source

§ This is for Spring 2.5.1. Check the documentation for other versions.

file in the classpath, but this could just have easily used a filesystem resource, a URL resource, or, if appropriate, a servlet context resource.

Spring beans written in a dynamic language require some features from the ApplicationContext interface, so a plain BeanFactory implementation such as that used in Example 4-11 won't work.

Example 4-11. Using JRuby within a BeanFactory won't work

```
package org.jrubycookbook.ch04;

import org.springframework.beans.factory.xml.XmlBeanFactory;
import org.springframework.core.io.ClassPathResource;

public class ListenerBootstrap {
    public static void main(String[] args) {
        ClassPathResource config =
            new ClassPathResource("org/jrubycookbook/ch04/listener_beans.xml");
        XmlBeanFactory ctx = new XmlBeanFactory(config);

        Listener listener = (Listener) ctx.getBean("rubyListener");
        listener.receiveMessage("Hello");
    }
}
```

Instead, we have to use an ApplicationContext implementation, such as the Class PathXmlApplicationContext class used in Example 4-12.

Example 4-12. Using JRuby within an ApplicationContext

```
package org.jrubycookbook.ch04;

import org.springframework.context.support.ClassPathXmlApplicationContext;

public class ListenerBootstrap {
    public static void main(String[] args) {
        String config = "org/jrubycookbook/ch04/listener_beans.xml";
        ClassPathXmlApplicationContext ctx =
            new ClassPathXmlApplicationContext(config);

        Listener listener = (Listener) ctx.getBean("rubyListener");
        listener.receiveMessage("Hello");
    }
}
```

Looking back at Example 4-10, you can see that this script both defines a Ruby class named RubyListener *and* returns a new instance of that class. This wasn't actually necessary in this case; Spring would be capable of recognizing that the script had created a class and would generate a new instance of that class if one had not been provided. However, it is good practice to include this command because Spring may not always create a new instance of the correct class. The best example of this is when the reference Ruby file contains multiple class definitions, as in Example 4-13.

Example 4-13. Ruby script that will confuse Spring

```ruby
class RubyListener
    def setPrefix(p)
        @prefix = p
    end

    # implementation of Listener interface
    def receiveMessage(s)
        puts "#{@prefix}Got Message: #{s}"
    end
end

class OtherRubyListener < RubyListener
    # implementation of Listener interface
    def receiveMessage(s)
        puts "#{@prefix}Got A Message: #{s}"
    end
end
```

As a result, it's simpler to always use the `new` command on the last line of your Ruby
script to ensure that Spring has access to the correct object.

See Also

- The Spring Framework website, *http://www.springframework.org/*

4.6 Creating Refreshable JRuby Spring Beans

Problem

Your Spring container includes beans that you want to reload when their underlying
definitions change.

Solution

Add a `refresh-check-delay` attribute to the `lang:jruby` element in your Spring XML
configuration file. The use of this attribute tells Spring to watch the resource referenced
in the `script-source` attribute. The value indicates how many milliseconds will pass
between scans of the resource for changes.

Alternatively, you can apply a default value for the refresh-check-delay attribute by
using the `defaults` element in the `lang` namespace. For example, to apply a one second
delay to all dynamic-language beans in the `ApplicationContext`, include this element in
your XML configuration file:

```xml
<lang:defaults refresh-check-delay="1000"/>
```

Discussion

One simple way to demonstrate this refreshable bean functionality is to use Spring's support for Java Timer objects. The Spring configuration XML in Example 4-14 includes the same `rubyListener` bean defined in Example 4-10 and adds an implementation of `java.util.TimerTask` to output the current time. It also includes the Spring plumbing necessary to invoke this task every five seconds.

Example 4-14. Refreshable JRuby Spring bean called by a TimerTask

```xml
<?xml version="1.0" encoding="UTF-8"?>
<beans xmlns="http://www.springframework.org/schema/beans"
    xmlns:xsi="http://www.w3.org/2001/XMLSchema-instance"
    xmlns:lang="http://www.springframework.org/schema/lang"
    xsi:schemaLocation="http://www.springframework.org/schema/beans
        http://www.springframework.org/schema/beans/spring-beans.xsd
        http://www.springframework.org/schema/lang
        http://www.springframework.org/schema/lang/spring-lang.xsd">

    <lang:defaults refresh-check-delay="1000" />

    <lang:jruby id="rubyListener"
        script-interfaces="org.jrubycookbook.ch04.Listener "
        script-source="classpath:org/jrubycookbook/ch04/ruby_listener.rb">
        <lang:property name="prefix" value="(from Timer) " />
    </lang:jruby>

    <bean id="sendDateTask" class="org.jrubycookbook.ch04.SendDateTask">
        <property name="listener" ref="rubyListener"/>
    </bean>

    <bean id="scheduledTask"
        class="org.springframework.scheduling.timer.ScheduledTimerTask">
        <property name="period" value="5000" />
        <property name="timerTask" ref="sendDateTask" />
    </bean>

    <bean id="timerFactory"
        class="org.springframework.scheduling.timer.TimerFactoryBean">
        <property name="scheduledTimerTasks">
            <list>
                <ref bean="scheduledTask" />
            </list>
        </property>
    </bean>
</beans>
```

The `SendDateTask` class, seen in Example 4-15, simply formats the current date and passes it to the injected implementation of the `Listener` interface.

Example 4-15. The SendDateTask class

```
package org.jrubycookbook.ch04;

import java.util.Date;
import java.util.TimerTask;

public class SendDateTask extends TimerTask {

    private Listener listener;

    public void setListener(Listener listener) {
        this.listener = listener;
    }

    public void run() {
        listener.receiveMessage(String.format("%tT", new Date()));
    }
}
```

With these classes in place, we can start up the `ApplicationContext` with the code in Example 4-16. Once it is running, changes to the *ruby_listener.rb* file can be seen with each execution of `SendDateTask`.

Example 4-16. Starting an ApplicationContext with Timer support

```
package org.jrubycookbook.ch04;

import org.springframework.context.support.ClassPathXmlApplicationContext;

public class TimedBootstrap {
    public static void main(String[] args) {
        String config = "org/jrubycookbook/ch04/timer_beans.xml";
        ClassPathXmlApplicationContext ctx =
            new ClassPathXmlApplicationContext(config);
    }
}
```

For example, we could change the `RubyListener` class to reverse the messages:

```
class RubyListener
    def setPrefix(p)
        @prefix = p
    end

    # implementation of Listener interface
    def receiveMessage(s)
        puts "#{@prefix}Got Message: #{s}".reverse
    end
end

RubyListener.new
```

Making this change while the `ApplicationContext` is running can produce output like this:

```
(from Timer) Got Message: 21:21:48
(from Timer) Got Message: 21:21:53
85:12:12 :egasseM toG )remiT morf(
```

4.7 Defining JRuby Spring Beans Inline

Problem

You're using Spring and want to define beans in JRuby directly inside your Spring XML configuration file instead of in an external file.

Solution

Instead of providing a resource location with a `script-source` attribute, you can include JRuby script inside an `inline-script` element in the `lang` namespace as seen in Example 4-17.

Example 4-17. JRuby script inside an inline-script element

```
<?xml version="1.0" encoding="UTF-8"?>
<beans xmlns="http://www.springframework.org/schema/beans"
    xmlns:xsi="http://www.w3.org/2001/XMLSchema-instance"
    xmlns:lang="http://www.springframework.org/schema/lang"
    xsi:schemaLocation="http://www.springframework.org/schema/beans
        http://www.springframework.org/schema/beans/spring-beans.xsd
        http://www.springframework.org/schema/lang
        http://www.springframework.org/schema/lang/spring-lang.xsd">

    <lang:jruby id="rubyListener"
        script-interfaces="org.jrubycookbook.ch04.Listener">
        <lang:inline-script><![CDATA[
class RubyListener
    def setPrefix(p)
        @prefix = p
    end

    # implementation of Listener interface
    def receiveMessage(s)
        puts "#{@prefix}Got Message: #{s}"
    end
end

RubyListener.new
        ]]></lang:inline-script>
        <lang:property name="prefix" value="(from Ruby) " />
    </lang:jruby>

</beans>
```

4.8 Applying Spring-Aware Interfaces to JRuby Objects

Problem

Your Spring `ApplicationContext` contains JRuby-based beans that need to implement one of the `Aware` interfaces, such as `org.springframework.context.Application ContextAware`.

Solution

Include implementations of the methods defined in the interface in your JRuby class and add the appropriate interface name to the `script-interfaces` attribute.

Discussion

The Spring Framework includes a number of interfaces that can be used to make a bean aware of its surroundings. Generally, these interfaces define a single method that is called by the container during initialization. Here is a sampling of these interfaces:

`org.springframework.context.ApplicationContextAware`
> The `ApplicationContext` instance that contains this bean is passed to the `setApplicationContext()` method.

`org.springframework.beans.factory.BeanFactoryAware`
> The `BeanFactory` instance that contains this bean is passed to the `set BeanFactory()` method.

`org.springframework.beans.factory.BeanNameAware`
> The name of this bean in the containing `BeanFactory` is passed to the `setBean Name()` method.

`org.springframework.context.ResourceLoaderAware`
> A `ResourceLoader`, which can resolve a `String` identifier to a `Resource` object, is passed to the `setResourceLoader()` method.

`org.springframework.context.MessageSourceAware`
> A `MessageSource`, which can resolve a message code and parameters to an appropriately internationalized message, is passed to the `setMessageSource()` method.

`org.springframework.web.context.ServletContextAware`
> A `javax.servlet.ServletContext` object is passed to the `setServletContext()` method.

Example 4-18 shows an inline implementation of the `BeanNameAware` interface.

Example 4-18. Inline JRuby Spring bean that implements the BeanNameAware interface

```
<lang:jruby id="rubyListener"
    script-interfaces="org.jrubycookbook.ch04.Listener,
            org.springframework.beans.factory.BeanNameAware">
    <lang:inline-script><![CDATA[
```

```
class RubyListener
    # implementation of BeanNameAware interface
    def setBeanName(beanName)
        @beanName = beanName
    end

    # implementation of Listener interface
    def receiveMessage(s)
        puts "Hello, I'm named #{@beanName}"
        puts "#{@prefix}Got Message: #{s}"
    end
end

RubyListener.new
    ]]></lang:inline-script>
</lang:jruby>
```

As implementations of these interfaces are generally the same—just save the injected object into an instance variable—they are a good case for using Ruby modules. Example 4-19 contains a Ruby module named Spring that includes boilerplate implementations of the interfaces listed earlier in this recipe.

Example 4-19. Ruby module implementing Spring aware interfaces

```
module Spring
    # implementation of ApplicationContextAware interface
    module ApplicationContextAware
        def setApplicationContext(ctx)
            @applicationContext = ctx
        end
    end

    # implementation of BeanFactoryAware interface
    module BeanFactoryAware
        def setBeanFactory(bf)
            @beanFactory = bf
        end
    end

    # implementation of BeanNameAware interface
    module BeanNameAware
        def setBeanName(beanName)
            @beanName = beanName
        end
    end

    # implementation of ResourceLoaderAware interface
    module ResourceLoaderAware
        def setResourceLoader(loader)
            @resourceLoader = loader
        end
    end

    # implementation of MessageSourceAware interface
    module MessageSourceAware
```

```ruby
        def setMessageSource(source)
            @messageSource = source
        end
    end

    # implementation of ServletContextAware interface
    module ServletContextAware
        def setServletContext(ctx)
            @servletContext = ctx
        end
    end
end
```

Using this module in a Ruby class is simply a matter of including the appropriate module, as in Example 4-20.

Example 4-20. Using a Spring module

```ruby
require "spring.rb"

class RubyListener
    include Spring::BeanNameAware

    # implementation of Listener interface
    def receiveMessage(s)
        puts "Hello, I'm named #{@beanName}"
        puts "#{@prefix}Got Message: #{s}"
    end
end
```

Determining JRuby's Load Path

Once you start including external files in your JRuby scripts, as in Example 4-20, it becomes critical to have a handle on your load path. Depending on how you invoke JRuby, the load path may be different when JRuby is used inside the Spring container than when JRuby is run from the command line. Here is a simple JRuby Spring bean that will output the load path when the container loads:

```xml
<lang:jruby id="loadPathOutputter" script-interfaces=\
"org.springframework.beans.factory.InitializingBean">
    <lang:inline-script><![CDATA[
class LoadPathOutputter
    def afterPropertiesSet()
        puts "Ruby Path is #{$:.join(';')}"
    end
end

LibOutputter.new
    ]]></lang:inline-script>
</lang:jruby>
```

You can use the `java.home` system property to change JRuby's load path. See Recipe 3.1 for details.

See Also

- Recipe 3.1, "Executing Ruby from Java"

4.9 Creating Spring MVC Controllers with JRuby

Problem

Redeploying a Java controller in Spring MVC can be time-consuming and disruptive to development. This is especially the case for web applications with many modules and/or large amounts of data loaded on startup. You would like to modify your controller code without reloading the running web application.

Solution

Spring's dynamic language support can speed up the development of Spring MVC applications by allowing you to define the controllers as JRuby objects. Not only can you eliminate the compilation step needed for Java development, but with Spring's refreshable bean feature (see Recipe 4.5), controller classes can be updated and redefined at runtime without a redeployment of the full web application. Open the Spring configuration file and create a JRuby controller by defining a Spring bean using the dynamic language elements as described in Recipe 4.4 and Recipe 4.5. Set the value of `script-interfaces` to `org.springframework.web.servlet.mvc.Controller` and `script-source` to the location of a Ruby file that will define and instantiate the controller class. Note that the `scripts-source` value is relative to the web application folder. Example 4-21 shows a Spring configuration file with a JRuby controller named `hellocontroller` that renders a JSP page.

Example 4-21. Spring configuration file with simple JRuby controller

```
<beans xmlns="http://www.springframework.org/schema/beans"
  xmlns:xsi="http://www.w3.org/2001/XMLSchema-instance"
  xmlns:lang="http://www.springframework.org/schema/lang"
  xsi:schemaLocation="http://www.springframework.org/schema/beans
http://www.springframework.org/schema/beans/spring-beans-2.5.xsd
http://www.springframework.org/schema/lang
http://www.springframework.org/schema/lang/spring-lang-2.5.xsd">

  <lang:jruby id="hellocontroller" refresh-check-delay="3000"
    script-source="/WEB-INF/ruby/hello.rb"
    script-interfaces="org.springframework.web.servlet.mvc.Controller">
  </lang:jruby>

  <bean id="viewResolver"
    class="org.springframework.web.servlet.view.InternalResourceViewResolver">
    <property name="viewClass"
      value="org.springframework.web.servlet.view.JstlView"/>
    <property name="prefix" value="/WEB-INF/jsp/"/>
    <property name="suffix" value=".jsp"/>
```

```
    </bean>

    <bean id="urlMapping"
        class="org.springframework.web.servlet.handler.SimpleUrlHandlerMapping">
        <property name="mappings">
            <props>
                <prop key="/hello.htm">hellocontroller</prop>
            </props>
        </property>
    </bean>
</beans>
```

Open the Ruby file specified by the `script-source` value and create a JRuby class with a `handleRequest` method that takes two arguments, the `HttpServletRequest` and `HttpServletResponse` objects. The `handleRequest` method is called on each web request and returns a Java `ModelAndView` object that contains the view name and model map. The last statement in your Ruby file must instantiate the new controller class. Example 4-22 shows a JRuby controller that adds a few values to the model and renders the *hello.jsp* template.

Example 4-22. JRuby class as a Spring MVC controller

```
include Java

import org.springframework.web.servlet.ModelAndView

class HelloController
    def handleRequest(request, response)
        mav = ModelAndView.new "hello"
        mav.add_object("example","hello!")
        mav.add_object("example_hash",{"foo"=>"bar","alpha"=>"beta"})
        return mav
    end
end

HelloController.new
```

The JSP page in Example 4-23 uses the standard syntax to access the model data and works independently from the controller's choice of implementation language. The Ruby hash that was added to the model, `example_hash`, is conveniently converted into a Java map and accessed using the JSP shorthand for outputting maps.

Example 4-23. Simple JSP template

```
<%@ page contentType="text/html;charset=UTF-8" language="java" %>

<!DOCTYPE html PUBLIC "-//W3C//DTD HTML 4.01 Transitional//EN"
    "http://www.w3.org/TR/html4/loose.dtd">
<html>
    <head>
        <meta http-equiv="Content-Type" content="text/html; charset=ISO-8859-1">
        <title>My Sample JSP</title>
    </head>
```

```
  <body>
    String val: ${example}<br/>
    Hash val foo: ${example_hash.foo}<br/>
    Hash val moo: ${example_hash.alpha}<br/>
  </body>
</html>
```

Redeploy your controller by overwriting the existing Ruby file in your web application. Update the file in the web application folder if you are deploying an expanded WAR. Otherwise, locate the temporary folder where the container has exploded your WAR or EAR file and update the controller. Consult the documentation of your application server because this location differs for each server and platform; it is usually found in a temporary file area or in the same folder as the WAR. The location of the expanded WAR is often written to the console on startup and can be found in the application server's logs.

Discussion

JRuby controllers can also be defined in your Spring configuration file using the inline bean support (see Recipe 4.5). The `inlinecontroller` bean in Example 4-24 contains the same code that would normally be in the Ruby file specified by the **script-source** value. It's not advised to build your entire web application using this technique for code management reasons and the loss of the redeployment feature, but this feature may be useful for the quick prototyping of controllers or adding some simple redirection logic, which is demonstrated in Example 4-24.

Example 4-24. Inline JRuby controller definition

```
<lang:jruby id="inlinecontroller"
  script-interfaces="org.springframework.web.servlet.mvc.Controller">
    <lang:inline-script>
include Java
import org.springframework.web.servlet.ModelAndView
class MySecController
   def handleRequest(request, response)
      ModelAndView.new "redirect:/hello.htm"
   end
end
MySecController.new
  </lang:inline-script>
</lang:jruby>
```

See Also

- Recipe 4.5, "Defining Spring Beans in JRuby"
- Recipe 4.6, "Creating Refreshable JRuby Spring Beans"
- Recipe 4.7, "Defining JRuby Spring Beans Inline"

4.10 Using Hibernate with JRuby

Problem

You would like to use Hibernate in your JRuby application.

Solution

Ideally, working with a Hibernate Data Access Object (DAO) should be no different from any other Java class. The main concern for JRuby developers is the use of Java Generics and JRuby's inability to create classes or call methods with input arguments that use the Generics feature. Hibernate gives Java developers a lot of flexibility in the implementation of the DAO and many leverage Java Generics to reduce the size of classes and method counts. However, the typical pattern for creating DAOs in the most popular online tutorials do not expose the Generics as part of the DAOs' public API, even though they are used internally. They are commonly created through a factory interface or by instantiating wrapper DAOs for classes. The JRuby program in Example 4-25 accesses the `PersonDao` through a factory while the `EventDao` is directly instantiated.

Example 4-25. Accessing Hibernate Data Access Objects

```
include Java

import example.dao.PersonDao
import example.dao.DaoFactory
import example.dao.EventDao
import example.model.Person
import example.model.Event
import util.HibernateUtil

event_dao = EventDao.new
event_dao.set_session HibernateUtil::get_session_factory.get_current_session
dao.create(Event.new("JRuby Meeting",java.util.Date.new))
dao.find_all.each do |e| puts "#{e.get_title } #{e.get_date}"; end

person_dao = DaoFactory.instantiate(PersonDao.class)
dao.create(Person.new("Justin","Wood"))
dao.create(Person.new("Brian","Henry"))
dao.find_all.each do |p| puts "#{p.get_firstname} #{p.get_lastname}"; end
```

Discussion

The Hibernate session is obtained through a static method in the `HibernateUtil` class and manually injected into the `EventDao` class. It's a common Hibernate design pattern to provide access to the Hibernate session factory through a static method in a global utility class. The `HibernateUtil` class becomes the common point of configuration and management and can hide many of the mapping details from your DAOs.

Database transactions can be nicely expressed using a Ruby function that yields to an inputted block. The block contains the database interaction code and is evaluated between the enclosing parent function's call to initialize and end the transaction. Errors can be detected and handled in the transaction function and kept out of the business code. The result is clean API that eliminates the verbose and repetitive transaction calls and an enhanced clarity of the transactional code, which is now identified through a function metaphor rather than explicit API calls to begin and end the transaction. Example 4-26 defines a `TransactionHelper` module that contains functions to initiate a standard JDBC transaction and the more universal Java Transaction API (JTA) transaction. The example also includes a controller that demonstrates the use of the module and how to easily add either transaction mechanism to your database access code.

Example 4-26. Using blocks to define transactions

```
include Java

import util.HibernateUtil
import javax.naming.InitialContext

module TransactionHelper

  def with_transaction
    begin
      tx = HibernateUtil.session_factory.current_session.beginTransaction
      yield
      tx.commit
      HibernateUtil.session_factory.current_session.close
    rescue
      tx.rollback
    end
  end

  def with_jta_transaction
    begin
      ctx = InitialContext.new
      utx = ctx.lookup("java:comp/UserTransaction");
      utx.begin();
      yield
      utx.commit
    rescue
      utx.rollback
    end
  end
end

class UserController
    extend TransactionHelper
  def create
    with_transaction do
      @id = User.create("Tom")
    end

    with_jta_transaction do
```

```
        tom = User.find_by_id(@id)
      end
    end
end
```

4.11 Using the Java Persistence API with JRuby

Problem

You want to use the Java Persistence API (JPA) in your JRuby application.

Solution

Use the static JPA method `Persistence.createEntityManagerFactory()` to generate a factory for your persistence unit. A call to the factory's `createEntityManager()` method generates a new `EntityManager` class, which is your primary tool for accessing the Persistence API. The `EntityManager` is analogous to Hibernate's `Session` or Toplink's `ClientSession` object and contains the methods to interact with the database and your model objects. The `EntityManager` object is not threadsafe and shouldn't be used with multiple concurrent requests. It is designed to be used and discarded in a relatively short amount of time and not as a long-running software component. Example 4-27 shows a JRuby application that creates a few `User` objects and then queries the database to confirm that they were successfully added.

Example 4-27. Example JPA access from JRuby

```
include Java

import javax.persistence.Persistence
import cookbook.User

def with_trans(em)
 t = em.getTransaction();
 begin
   t.begin()
   yield
   t.commit
 ensure
   t.rollback if t.isActive
 end
end

emf = Persistence.createEntityManagerFactory("hello-world")
em = emf.createEntityManager

with_trans(em) do
     u = User.new("stephen","lee","slee","password","stephen@ora.com")
     u2 = User.new("stephen","smith","ssmith","password","ssmith@ora.com")
     em.persist(u)
     em.persist(u2)
end
```

```
query = em.createQuery("select u from User u where u.firstname = :firstname").
query.set_parameter("firstname", "stephen").
hu = query.get_result_list

hu.each do |u|
  puts "found #{u.firstname} #{u.lastname}"
end

em.close
emf.close
```

Discussion

The example demonstrates the use of a block once again (see Recipe 4.9) to express a
JPA transaction. This helper method also automatically rolls back the transaction if the
commit should fail.

See Also

- Recipe 4.10, "Using Hibernate with JRuby"

4.12 Making SOAP Calls

Credit: Steven Shingler

Problem

You need to invoke a remote method through a SOAP-based web service.

Solution

Use the Mule client module, available from *http://mule.mulesource.org*, and a Ruby
XML parsing library such as REXML or Hpricot. Example 4-28 uses Mule to make a
request to one of the web services provided by the National Oceanic and Atmospheric
Administration (NOAA).

Example 4-28. Making a SOAP request with the Mule client module

```
include Java

require "rexml/document"
import org.mule.module.client.MuleClient

url = "axis:http://www.weather.gov/forecasts/xml/SOAP_server/ndfdXMLserver.php"
method = "method=LatLonListZipCode"
client = MuleClient.new
message = client.send("#{url}?#{method}", "10036", nil)
doc = REXML::Document.new message.payload
puts doc.root.elements[1].text
exit
```

To run this script, Mule and several dependencies need to be added to the classpath. Because of classloader requirements, these dependencies must be on the system classpath (e.g., through the use of the CLASSPATH environment variable); they cannot be added to the classpath by using JRuby's extension of the require method as described in Recipe 1.7. For this particular script, the dependencies can be added to the classpath using these commands:

```
export MULE_LIB=/opt/mule/lib
export CLASSPATH=$CLASSPATH:$MULE_LIB/opt/activation-1.1.jar
export CLASSPATH=$CLASSPATH:$MULE_LIB/opt/axis-1.4.jar
export CLASSPATH=$CLASSPATH:$MULE_LIB/opt/axis-jaxrpc-1.4.jar
export CLASSPATH=$CLASSPATH:$MULE_LIB/opt/backport-util-concurrent-3.1.jar
export CLASSPATH=$CLASSPATH:$MULE_LIB/opt/commons-beanutils-1.7.0.jar
export CLASSPATH=$CLASSPATH:$MULE_LIB/opt/commons-codec-1.3.jar
export CLASSPATH=$CLASSPATH:$MULE_LIB/opt/commons-collections-3.2.jar
export CLASSPATH=$CLASSPATH:$MULE_LIB/opt/commons-discovery-0.2.jar
export CLASSPATH=$CLASSPATH:$MULE_LIB/opt/commons-httpclient-3.1.jar
export CLASSPATH=$CLASSPATH:$MULE_LIB/opt/commons-io-1.3.1.jar
export CLASSPATH=$CLASSPATH:$MULE_LIB/opt/commons-lang-2.3.jar
export CLASSPATH=$CLASSPATH:$MULE_LIB/opt/commons-logging-1.1.1.jar
export CLASSPATH=$CLASSPATH:$MULE_LIB/opt/commons-pool-1.4.jar
export CLASSPATH=$CLASSPATH:$MULE_LIB/opt/dom4j-1.6.1.jar
export CLASSPATH=$CLASSPATH:$MULE_LIB/opt/geronimo-j2ee-connector_1.5_spec-1.1.jar
export CLASSPATH=$CLASSPATH:$MULE_LIB/opt/geronimo-servlet_2.5_spec-1.1.jar
export CLASSPATH=$CLASSPATH:$MULE_LIB/opt/jaxen-1.1.1.jar
export CLASSPATH=$CLASSPATH:$MULE_LIB/opt/jug-2.0.0-asl.jar
export CLASSPATH=$CLASSPATH:$MULE_LIB/mule/mule-core-2.0.2.jar
export CLASSPATH=$CLASSPATH:$MULE_LIB/mule/mule-module-client-2.0.2.jar
export CLASSPATH=$CLASSPATH:$MULE_LIB/mule/mule-transport-axis-2.0.2.jar
export CLASSPATH=$CLASSPATH:$MULE_LIB/opt/saaj-api-1.3.jar
export CLASSPATH=$CLASSPATH:$MULE_LIB/opt/stax-api-1.0.1.jar
export CLASSPATH=$CLASSPATH:$MULE_LIB/opt/wsdl4j-1.6.1.jar
export CLASSPATH=$CLASSPATH:$MULE_LIB/opt/wstx-asl-3.2.6.jar
```

 The "Full Distribution" Mule download includes all third-party dependencies except for Jakarta Commons Logging, which can be downloaded from *http://commons.apache.org/logging/*.

Discussion

The send method of the MuleClient class will accept any object as the message payload. However, care must be taken when passing objects other than Java primitives or their Ruby equivalents. For these other types, use the Axis WSDL2Java tool to generate Java classes from the web service's descriptor:

```
$ java org.apache.axis.wsdl.WSDL2Java\
http://www.weather.gov/forecasts/xml/SOAP_server/ndfdXMLserver.php?wsdl
```

In Example 4-28, the URL for the NOAA web service endpoint is prefixed with axis, indicating to the Mule engine that we wish to use the Axis library to invoke the web service. By including different and/or additional dependencies on the classpath, different libraries and different transport mechanisms can be used.

See Also

- Mule website, *http://mule.mulesource.org/*
- Apache Axis website, *http://ws.apache.org/axis/*
- REXML website, *http://www.germane-software.com/software/rexml/*
- Hpricot website, *http://code.whytheluckystiff.net/hpricot/*

4.13 Simplifying LDAP Access

Problem

You are looking up entries and attributes in an LDAP directory through JNDI and are looking to simplify the API.

Solution

Use JRuby's open class feature (described in Recipe 1.9) to add helper methods to the `com.sun.jndi.ldap.LdapCtx` class.

Discussion

Although powerful, the JNDI API can frequently feel unnecessarily verbose. For example, the Java code required to access a single attribute value is awkward:

```
// Lookup the entry
LdapContext entry = ctx.lookup("uid=mts,ou=People,dc=umich,dc=edu");
// First, get all of the Attributes associated with this entry.
Attributes attributes = entry.getAttributes("");
// Then get a single named Attribute.
Attribute attribute = attributes.get("mail");
// Then actually get the value.
String value = (String) attribute.get();
```

For an attribute with multiple values, it's even worse:

```
// Lookup the entry
LdapContext entry = ctx.lookup("uid=mts,ou=People,dc=umich,dc=edu");
// First, get all of the Attributes associated with this entry.
Attributes attributes = entry.getAttributes("");
// Then get a single named Attribute.
Attribute attribute = attributes.get("mail");
// Then get a NamingEnumeration of the attribute values.
NamingEnumeration ne = attribute.getAll();
// Create a list, loop through the NamingEnumeration,
// and add each value to the list
List<String> values = new ArrayList<String>();
while (ne.hasMore()) {
```

```
        values.add(ne.next());
    }
```

Example 4-29 shows two methods being added to the `LdapCtx` class, which simplify this API significantly.

Example 4-29. Adding methods to the LdapCtx class

```
include Java

import com.sun.jndi.ldap.LdapCtx

class LdapCtx
    def get_attribute_value(key)
        get_attributes("", [key].to_java(:string)).get(key).get
    end
    def get_attribute_values(key)
        values = []
        enum = get_attributes("", [key].to_java(:string)).get(key).get_all
        while enum.has_more
            values << enum.next
        end
        return values
    end
end
```

Adding these methods makes the following code to access the LDAP attributes:

```
entry = ctx.lookup("uid=mts,ou=People,dc=umich,dc=edu")

p "Email = #{entry.get_attribute_value("mail")}"
entry.get_attribute_values("cn").each do |name|
    p "Name = #{name}"
end
```

For Example 4-29 to work, you must use Sun's LDAP JNDI support from the package `com.sun.ldap.jndi`. Typically, this is done by creating a JNDI `Context`, as shown in Recipe 4.1. If you are using a different LDAP library, you can easily adapt the listing in Example 4-29 to the library. All you need to do is discover the name of the class that implements `javax.naming.directory.DirContext`. You can easily use `jirb` for this:

```
$ jirb
irb(main):001:0> include Java
irb(main):002:0> import java.util.Hashtable
irb(main):003:0> import javax.naming.InitialContext
irb(main):004:0> import javax.naming.Context
irb(main):005:0> env = {
irb(main):006:1*     Context::INITIAL_CONTEXT_FACTORY,
irb(main):007:1*     "com.sun.jndi.ldap.LdapCtxFactory",
irb(main):008:1* Context::PROVIDER_URL,
irb(main):009:1* "ldap://ldap.itd.umich.edu:389"
irb(main):010:1> }
irb(main):011:0> ctx = InitialContext.new(Hashtable.new(env))
irb(main):012:0> ctx.lookup("uid=mts,ou=People,dc=umich,dc=edu").java_class
=> com.sun.jndi.ldap.LdapCtx
```

## CHAPTER 5

User Interface and Graphics

5.0 Introduction

The JRuby community has paid a lot of attention to web development, but JRuby is also a powerful tool for client application development. By allowing the runtime to access the graphics subsystem, JRuby can be used to create GUI applications with the Abstract Windowing Toolkit (AWT), Swing and the Simple Widget Toolkit (SWT), as well as newer projects like Qt Jambi. These toolkits have a rich set of UI widgets but they also permit tight integration with the native operating system. A few recipes in this chapter explain how to use JRuby to create system tray and desktop components and access native GUI libraries.

Given the popularity of declarative programming and Ruby's powerful Domain-Specific Language (DSL) building capabilities, it is to be expected that JRuby developers would explore ways to improve traditional Java UI programming. There are several options to facilitate Swing development: Swigby, Cheri::Swing, Monkeybars, and Profligacy. Similarly, the Glimmer Eclipse project was created for SWT and QT::JRuby has built-in DSL support.

The Rawr gem is a useful tool for packaging your JRuby applications desktop as well as the Web. This gem provides a set of Rake tasks that can be configured to package your JRuby programs as executable JAR files, Windows executables, Mac OS X applications, and Web Start applications. A recipe also describes techniques for using JRuby to build Java applets.

Image processing is one of the few areas where Ruby runtimes still depend on native or C code. Use RMagic4J and ImageVoodoo as alternatives to the popular RMagic and ImageScience gems. You can also access the Java 2D API for advanced processing needs.

5.1 Creating Swing Applications

Problem

You want to build your Java Swing user interface with JRuby.

Solution

JRuby's runtime support extends to the graphics libraries and Swing components. Example 5-1 shows a simple Swing application that displays a message in a window.

Example 5-1. Simple Swing UI

```
include Java
import javax.swing.JFrame

frame = JFrame.new "JRuby Message"
frame.default_close_operation = JFrame::EXIT_ON_CLOSE
msg = javax.swing.JLabel.new "JRuby Rocks"
frame.content_pane.add msg
frame.pack
frame.visible = true
```

Discussion

JRuby can access the entire Swing API, including advanced features like the Look and Feel libraries. Example 5-2 shows how to toggle between Swing's default Metal theme and the native platform's Look and Feel.

Example 5-2. Changing the application's look and feel

```
include Java

import javax.swing.JFrame
import javax.swing.UIManager

frame = JFrame.new "JRuby Look And Feel"
frame.default_close_operation = JFrame::EXIT_ON_CLOSE
frame.content_pane.layout = java.awt.GridLayout.new(1, 2)

{:metal => "javax.swing.plaf.metal.MetalLookAndFeel",
 :system => UIManager::getSystemLookAndFeelClassName}.each do |l,c|
 but = javax.swing.JButton.new l.to_s
 but.add_action_listener do |evt|
    UIManager::look_and_feel = c
    javax.swing.SwingUtilities::updateComponentTreeUI frame
    frame.pack
 end
 frame.add(but)
end

frame.pack
frame.visible = true
```

You can access third-party Look and Feel libraries such as Substance or Napkin by including their JAR files in the Java classpath and referencing the name of the Look and Feel class.

See Also

- Recipe 5.2, "Swing Event Handling"
- Recipe 5.3, "Long-Running Tasks in Swing Applications"

5.2 Swing Event Handling

Problem

You want to handle events that are generated by Swing components.

Solution

You generally want to use the block coercion feature in JRuby for most GUI event processing. Event listeners that define only a single method such as `javax.awt.event.ActionListener` can make use of this feature and allow for very concise event-handling code. The application in Example 5-3 uses blocks to capture the button click event and changes to the text field.

Example 5-3. Events handled through block coercion

```
include Java
import javax.swing.JFrame

frame = JFrame.new "Event Handler - Coerced"
frame.default_close_operation = JFrame::EXIT_ON_CLOSE

t = javax.swing.JTextField.new(10)
b = javax.swing.JButton.new("search")
b.add_action_listener { |evt| puts "searching" };
t.document.add_document_listener { |evt| puts "checking #{t.text}" };

frame.layout = java.awt.GridLayout.new(1, 2)
frame.add t
frame.add b
frame.pack
frame.visible = true
```

Discussion

You can also instantiate the listener's Java interface using the `impl` method, passing a block inside which the event is handled. This approach is useful when the event handler interface contains multiple methods. Example 5-4 shows how to intercept events from the menu component.

Example 5-4. Events handled through an instance of a Java interface

```
include Java
import javax.swing.JFrame

frame = JFrame.new
frame.default_close_operation = JFrame::EXIT_ON_CLOSE

bar = javax.swing.JMenuBar.new
menu = javax.swing.JMenu.new "File"
item = javax.swing.JMenuItem.new "Open"

menu.add_menu_listener(javax.swing.event.MenuListener.impl do |method, evt|
  puts evt.class
  case method.to_s
    when "menuDeselected"
        puts 'hidden'
    when "menuSelected"
        puts 'visible'
  end
end)

menu.add item
bar.add menu
frame.jmenu_bar = bar
frame.pack
frame.visible = true
```

See Also

- Recipe 1.9, "Implementing a Java Interface in Ruby"

5.3 Long-Running Tasks in Swing Applications

Problem

The Swing event dispatching thread is responsible for drawing the user interface and event handling. You want to execute a long-running task that is initiated from a Swing event but allow the interface to remain responsive and active.

Solution

The class `javax.swing.SwingWorker` is designed to run long-running jobs while allowing for safe UI updates within the event dispatch thread. The implementation has evolved over the years through several open source projects and publications and was formally added to the core Java library in Java 6. To use **SwingWorker**, you first create a new class that extends **SwingWorker**. Next, implement the required **doInBackground** method with your long-running action. Example 5-5 shows **SwingWorker** in action. Note that the button component is a member of the worker class because the variable is not accessible within the scope of the new class.

Example 5-5. Using the SwingWorker for long-running jobs

```
include Java
import javax.swing.JFrame

frame = JFrame.new "Swing Worker"
frame.default_close_operation = JFrame::EXIT_ON_CLOSE

start = javax.swing.JButton.new("start")

#define the function using a block
start.add_action_listener do |evt|
  class MySwingWorker < javax.swing.SwingWorker
    attr_accessor :button
    def doInBackground
      10.times do
        puts "thread #{self.hashCode} working"
        sleep(1)
      end
      self.button.text = "Completed"
    end
  end

  sw = MySwingWorker.new
  sw.button = start
  sw.execute
end

frame.add start
frame.pack
frame.visible = true
```

Discussion

As of version 1.1, JRuby cannot instantiate abstract Java classes, so you must subclass `SwingWorker` to provide the implementation of the abstract methods. This is one of the few areas were JRuby results in less fluid and elegant code than its Java counterpart, but the JRuby team is working on improving support for abstract classes in future versions of JRuby.

`SwingWorker` has optional methods that provide advanced features, such as incremental job progress, job cancellation, and completion detection. Explore the API and overload the optional methods in your Ruby class to use these features.

There is a version of `SwingWorker` for Java 5 that is conceptually similar to the Java 6 version, but does not make use of Java generics and uses slightly different method names. For example, the construct method in the Java 5 class is analogous to the `doBackground` method in the Java 6's `SwingWorker`.

See Also

- Recipe 1.9, "Implementing a Java Interface in Ruby"
- Java 5 `SwingWorker`, *http://java.sun.com/products/jfc/tsc/articles/threads/src/Swing Worker.java*

5.4 Packaging Standalone Applications

Problem

You want to package your JRuby application as an executable JAR file, Windows executable, or Mac OS X application.

Solution

Install the Rawr gem. This gem was created by David Koontz to simplify the packaging of JRuby applications for Windows, Mac, Linux, and Java environments:

```
$ jruby -S gem install rawr
```

Set up the Rawr build environment by running the `rawr install` command in your build folder, usually the top level of your project folder:

```
$ cd /projects/rawrdemo
$ jruby -S rawr install
```

This command creates two files: *build_configuration.yaml* and *src/org/rubyforge/rawr/ Main.java*, a Java class that instantiates a JRuby runtime and executes your Ruby application's script. Copy your JRuby application's files into the newly created *src* folder. If your project depends upon custom Java classes, package those class files into a JAR file and place your project JAR file along with any JAR files upon which your application depends in the *lib/java* folder. You must also have the *jruby-complete.jar* file in the *lib/ java* folder.

Open the *build_configuration.yaml* file and set the `project_name` parameter to the name you would like for the final executable. Change the `main_ruby_file` parameter to the application's main execution script name or rename the file to the default script name, *main.rb*. Example 5-6 shows a sample configuration file.

Example 5-6. Example Rawr configuration file

```
# Name of the created jar file
project_name: jruby_cookbook_app

# Ruby file to invoke when jar is started
main_ruby_file: jruby_cookbook_main
```

Executable JAR

Run the `rawr:jar` Rake task to generate an executable JAR file:

```
$ jruby -S rake rawr:jar
```

The resulting files can found in the *package/deploy* directory. This includes the main executable JAR file *jruby_cookbook_app.jar*, a configuration file, and the JRuby runtime JAR file. You will need to include all the files in the folder along with the JAR files when you distribute your application. To test the JAR file, run:

```
$ java -jar package/deploy/jruby_cookbook_app.jar
```

Windows executable

Run the `rawr:bundle:exe` Rake task to generate a Windows executable:

```
$ jruby -S rake rawr:bundle:exe
```

The Windows application is composed of an *exe* file, several JAR files, and a configuration file found in the *package/native_deploy/windows* directory. Distribute and install the entire contents of the folder and not just the *exe* file.

Mac OS X application

Run the `rawr:bundle:app` Rake task to create a Mac OS X application:

```
$ jruby -S rake rawr:bundle:app
```

The bundled OS X application folder is called *project_name.app* and can be found in the *package/native_deploy/mac* directory.

Discussion

The *build_configuration.yaml* file is well documented and contains many options to customize the build. There are parameters to set the build's classpath, the location of the Java and JRuby source files, library file paths, and the destination folder of the resulting executables. You can also include arbitrary data or media files in your application by setting the `jars_data_dirs` parameter.

Use Rake's `-T` flag to get a complete list of Rawr's tasks. The `rawr:clean` task would be a good task to run before each build to avoid bundling unwanted files.

```
$ jruby -S rake -T
rake rawr:bundle:app     # Bundles the jar from rawr:jar into a native Mac O...
rake rawr:bundle:exe     # Bundles the jar from rawr:jar into a native Windo...
rake rawr:bundle:web     # Bundles the jar from rawr:jar into a Java Web Sta...
rake rawr:clean          # Removes the output directory
rake rawr:compile        # Compiles all the Java source files in the directo...
rake rawr:jar            # Uses compiled output and creates an executable ja...
rake rawr:prepare        # Creates the output directory and sub-directories,...
rake rawr:setup_consts   # Sets up the various constants used by the Rawr bu...
```

See Also

- Recipe 3.1, "Executing Ruby from Java"
- Recipe 5.9, "Accessing the Native Desktop"
- Rawr website, *http://gitorious.org/projects/rawr*

5.5 Packaging JRuby Web Start Applications

Problem

You want to package your JRuby program as a Java Web Start application.

Solution

Install the Rawr gem. See Recipe 5.4 for instructions on how to use and configure the gem. Because of the Web Start security model and JRuby's use of the VM, the main JAR file and the JRuby runtime JAR file must be signed to run in the Web Start security sandbox. Start by generating a keystore file named *myKeystore* with the alias `myself`. Enter a password and other information when prompted:

```
$ keytool -genkey -keystore myKeystore -alias myself
Enter keystore password: dumbpassword
What is your first and last name?
  [Unknown]: Henry Liu
What is the name of your organizational unit?
  [Unknown]: Global Digital
What is the name of your organization?
  [Unknown]: MTV Networks
What is the name of your City or Locality?
  [Unknown]: New York
What is the name of your State or Province?
  [Unknown]: NY
What is the two-letter country code for this unit?
  [Unknown]: US
Is CN=Henry Liu, OU=Global Digital, O=MTV Networks, L=New York, ST=NY, C=US
correct?
  [no]: yes

Enter key password for <myself>
        (RETURN if same as keystore password):
```

Using your newly created keystore, create a self-signed certificate with the `selfcert` option:

```
$ keytool -selfcert -alias myself -keystore myKeystore
```

Edit the *build_configuration.yaml* file and create a hash named `web_start` containing the key `self_sign` with the value `true` and a `self_sign_passphrase` key whose value is set to the certificate's password. Create a hash named `jnlp` with the required values for codebase, description, vendor, and homepage_href. Example 5-7 shows how to define YAML hashes in your configuration file.

Example 5-7. Web Start parameters in Rawr configuration file

```
web_start: { self_sign: true, self_sign_passphrase: password }

jnlp: {
    codebase: http://localhost:8080,
    description: My Webstart Demo,
    vendor: Your Name,
    homepage_href: http://www.ora.com
        }
```

Sign the JRuby runtime JAR file and other included JAR files that access the native system, use network services, or produce security errors:

```
$ jarsigner -keystore myKeystore -storepass password lib/java/jruby-complete.jar
```

Run the `rawr:bundle:web` Rake task to generate your Web Start application:

```
$ jruby -S rake rawr:bundle:web
```

The application is found in the *package/native_deploy/web* directory. Move all the files to your web server's distribution folder and launch the web start application by opening JNLP file in your browser. For example, if your web server was running on `localhost` using port 8080, you would use the URL *http://localhost:8080/jruby_cookbook.jnlp*.

Discussion

You can use the `file://` URL prefix with the javaws tool to test your Web Start without having to use to the web server or browser. Set the **codebase** value to the deployment directory in your *build_configuration.yaml* file, as seen here, and rebuild your application:

```
codebase: file:///C:/rawrdemo/package/native_deploy/web
```

Launch your Web Start application with the javaws command:

```
$ javaws package\native_deploy\web\jruby_cookbook.jnlp
```

Remember to change the codebase value to a web address when you deploy your application.

See Also

- Recipe 5.4, "Packaging Standalone Applications"

5.6 Creating JRuby Applets

Problem

You want to create a Java applet using JRuby.

Solution

Working with an applet in JRuby is slightly different from creating a desktop application because the Ruby code cannot instantiate its own main application window but must add components to the parent applet's content pane. One possible solution, shown in Example 5-8, is to expose the content pane as a global variable to the JRuby runtime.

Example 5-8. JRuby applet with content pane in a global variable

JRubyApplet.java

```
package org.jrubycookbook;

import java.util.ArrayList;
import org.jruby.Ruby;
import org.jruby.javasupport.*;
import java.awt.Container;
import org.jruby.runtime.builtin.IRubyObject;
import org.jruby.runtime.*;

public class JrubyApplet extends javax.swing.JApplet {
    public void init(){
        Ruby runtime = JavaEmbedUtils.initialize(new ArrayList<String>());
        runtime.evalScriptlet("require \"java\"\nclass FreshForJava\nend\n");
        final IRubyObject blankRuby = runtime.evalScriptlet("FreshForJava.new");
        IRubyObject globValue = JavaUtil.convertJavaToRuby(runtime,
            this.getContentPane());
        globValue = Java.java_to_ruby(blankRuby, globValue, Block.NULL_BLOCK);
        GlobalVariable gv = new GlobalVariable(runtime, "$content_pane",
            globValue);
        runtime.defineVariable(gv);
        String bootRuby = "require 'appletmain' \n";
        runtime.evalScriptlet( bootRuby );
    }
}
```

appletmain.rb

```
include Java

import javax.swing.JPanel
import javax.swing.JButton

jp = JPanel.new
but = JButton.new("OK")
but.add_action_listener do |evt|
```

```
    puts "pressed"
end
jp.add(but)
$content_pane.add(jp)
```

Package the Ruby scripts with your Java classes into a JAR file and then reference that JAR file from inside an HTML `applet` tag. Include the *jruby-complete.jar* with the JRuby runtime along with your application JAR file through the `archive` parameter. Example 5-9 shows a sample `applet` tag to be used in an HTML page.

Example 5-9. Applet tag for a JRuby applet

```
<applet width="200" height="200" align="baseline"
    code="org.jrubycookbook.JrubyApplet.class"
    codebase="." pluginspage="http://java.sun.com/j2se/1.6.0/download.html"
        archive="jrubyapplet.jar,jruby-complete.jar">
</applet>
```

Java 6 update 10 introduced a new method of embedding an applet through a JavaScript call. This technique is shown in Example 5-10.

Example 5-10. JavaScript applet deployment

```
<script src="http://java.com/js/deployJava.js"></script>
<script>
  deployJava.runApplet({codebase:"",
    archive:"jruby-complete.jar,jrubyapplet.jar",
    code:"org.jruby.JRubyApplet.class",
    width:"320", Height:"400"}, null, "1.6");
</script>
```

Discussion

An alternate approach, shown in Example 5-11, is for the Swing `Panel` object to be created and returned from the JRuby script execution. The appearance and behavior of the user interface is defined by the `MyPanel` class found in the *appletmainclass.rb* file.

Example 5-11. JRuby applet, alternate implementation

JRubyApplet.java

```
public class JrubyApplet extends javax.swing.JApplet {
    public void init() {
        Ruby runtime = JavaEmbedUtils.initialize(Collections.emtpyList());
        String bootRuby = "require 'appletmainclass' \n MyPanel.new \n";
        IRubyObject ro = runtime.evalScriptlet(bootRuby);
        Container panel = (Container)JavaEmbedUtils.rubyToJava
(runtime, ro, Container.class);
        this.getContentPane().add(panel);
        this.setSize(100,100);
    }
}
```

appletmainclass.rb

```
include Java

class MyPanel < javax.swing.JPanel
  include_package 'javax.swing'

  def initialize
    super
    but = JButton.new("OK")
    but.add_action_listener do |evt|
      puts "pressed too"
    end
    add(but)
  end
end
```

The code becomes a bit simpler in a Java 6 or later environment with JSR-223 support. The Java-to-JRuby object delegation code is eliminated in Example 5-12, improving the readability of the code.

Example 5-12. JRuby applet using Java Scripting

```
package org.jrubycookbook;

import javax.script.ScriptEngine;
import javax.script.ScriptEngineManager;
import javax.script.ScriptException;
import java.awt.Container;

public class JrubyApplet extends javax.swing.JApplet {

    public void init(){
        ScriptEngine runtime = new ScriptEngineManager().getEngineByName("jruby");
        String bootRuby = "require 'main' \n MyPanel.new \n";
        try{
            Container c = (Container)runtime.eval(bootRuby);
            this.getContentPane().add(c);
            this.setSize(100,100);
        } catch(ScriptException e) {
            e.printStackTrace();}

    }
}
```

Example 5-13 shows how to make the applet's content pane available as a global variable through the JSR-223 API.

Example 5-13. Applet using Java Scripting and a global variable

```
public class JrubyApplet extends javax.swing.JApplet {

    public void init(){
        ScriptEngine runtime = new ScriptEngineManager().getEngineByName("jruby");
        runtime.put("content_pane",this.getContentPane());
        String bootRuby = "require 'mainpassed' \n";
```

```
        try{
            runtime.eval(bootRuby);
        } catch(ScriptException e) {
            e.printStackTrace();
        }
    }
}
```

See Also

- Recipe 3.3, "Invoking JRuby Through Java Scripting Support"

5.7 Manipulating Images

Problem

You want to resize or otherwise modify an image using JRuby.

Solution

Use a JRuby-compatible image library such as RMagick4J or ImageVoodoo for simple tasks like thumbnail generation. The Java 2D API can be used when you need more advanced image-processing capabilities.

RMagick4J

RMagick is a gem frequently used by Ruby developers for thumbnail generation or image editing but it requires the C-based ImageMagick libraries. RMagick4J was created so JRuby developers could work with the familiar API and allow their existing application to remain compatible RMagic applications. Start by installing the RMagick4J gem:

```
$ jruby -S gem install rmagick4j
```

Example 5-14 demonstrates a simple thumbnail-creation operation. It also shows how to make the library compatible with the RMagick gem by using a small amount of platform-detection code to load the correct gem before including the appropriate gem.

Example 5-14. Creating thumbnails with RMagick4J

```
require 'rubygems'
gem defined?(JRUBY_VERSION) ? 'rmagick4j' : 'rmagick'
require 'RMagick'
include Magick

img = Image.new "avatar.jpg"
thumb = img.resize(0.25)
thumb.write "avatar-thumb.jpg"
```

RMagick4J has implemented most, but not all, of the functions from the original RMagick gem. The team has stated though they have a goal to provide complete compatibility with the C-based RMagick gem in the future.

ImageVoodoo

ImageVoodoo was created by JRuby core team members Tom Enebo and Nick Sieger. Its original purpose was to be an API-compatible JRuby implementation of Ryan Davis's ImageScience library, another widely used Ruby library for image processing. Begin by installing the ImageVoodoo gem:

```
$ jruby -S gem install image_voodoo
```

Example 5-15 shows how to create a thumbnail image using the library.

Example 5-15. Creating thumbnails with ImageVoodoo

```
require 'image_voodoo'

ImageVoodoo.with_image('logo-240-480.jpg') do |img|
  img.thumbnail(240) do |img|
    img.save "logo-120-240.jpg"
  end
end
```

The ImageVoodoo gem includes the *image_science.rb* file to provide compatibility with existing ImageScience code. If you open the file, you'll see that `ImageScience` class simply references to the `ImageVoodoo` class. Example 5-16 shows how we can replace our ImageVoodoo references in Example 5-15 with the ImageScience-equivalent code. By using the `ImageScience` class name, the code is completely portable between a C-Ruby and JRuby interpreter.

Example 5-16. ImageScience example

```
require 'image_science'

ImageScience.with_image('logo-240-480.jpg') do |img|
  img.thumbnail(100) do |img|
    img.save "logo-120-240-imagescience.jpg"
  end
end
```

With each new version of the gem, the ImageVoodoo team has added additional image-processing capabilities to the library such as color conversion, brightness, and grayscale. Example 5-17 uses the new `from_url` method to load an image from the Web and then process that image through a series of filters. The `preview` method in the example opens the image in a window; this is a helpful tool for rapid debugging or tweaking filter settings.

Example 5-17. ImageVoodoo extended features

```
require 'image_voodoo'

ImageVoodoo.from_url("http://www.google.com/intl/en_ALL/images/logo.gif") do |img|
  img.adjust_brightness(1.4,30) do |img3|
    img3.greyscale do |img4|
      img4.negative do |img5|
        img5.preview
      end
    end
  end
end
```

Discussion

Use the Java 2D API for low-level or custom image processing. The code shown in Example 5-18 produces the highest quality thumbnail by utilizing a common softening technique. The quality comes at the expense of the CPU because of the additional necessary image processing.

Example 5-18. Java 2D API thumbnail generation

```
include Java

import java.awt.Image
import java.awt.image.BufferedImage
import java.awt.image.ConvolveOp

quality = 0.5
newWidth = 300
i = javax.swing.ImageIcon.new("source-image.jpg").image
newImg, i_w, i_h = nil, i.width, i.height

if (i_w > i_h)
 newImg = i.getScaledInstance(newWidth, (newWidth * i_h)/i_w, Image::SCALE_SMOOTH)
else
 newImg = i.getScaledInstance((newWidth * i_h)/i_w, newWidth, Image::SCALE_SMOOTH)
end
tmp =(javax.swing.ImageIcon.new(newImg)).image

# Create a BufferedImage for the filter.
bufferedImage = BufferedImage.new(tmp.width, tmp.height,BufferedImage::TYPE_INT_RGB)
g = bufferedImage.createGraphics()

g.color = java.awt.Color::white
g.fillRect(0, 0, tmp.width, tmp.height)
g.drawImage(tmp, 0, 0, nil)
g.dispose()

# Apply softening filter.
softFact = 0.05
softArray = [0, softFact, 0, softFact, 1-(softFact*4), softFact, 0, softFact, 0]
kernel = java.awt.image.Kernel.new(3, 3, softArray.to_java(:float))
op = ConvolveOp.new(kernel, ConvolveOp::EDGE_NO_OP, nil);
```

```
bufferedImage = op.filter(bufferedImage,nil)

# Write the file.
out = java.io.FileOutputStream.new("output.jpg")
encoder = com.sun.image.codec.jpeg.JPEGCodec::createJPEGEncoder(out)
param = encoder.getDefaultJPEGEncodeParam(bufferedImage)
param.setQuality(quality, true)
encoder.setJPEGEncodeParam(param)
encoder.encode(bufferedImage)
puts "finished"
```

See Also

- ImageScience website, *http://seattlerb.rubyforge.org/ImageScience.html*
- RMagick website, *http://rmagick.rubyforge.org/*
- RMagick4J website, *http://code.google.com/p/rmagick4j/*

5.8 Creating SWT Applications

Problem

You want to create SWT applications using JRuby. The Standard Widget Toolkit (SWT) is probably the most popular Java client technology after the AWT and Swing libraries. It is open source software and is best known as the user interface framework used throughout the Eclipse IDE.

Solution

Download the SWT library and include the *swt.jar* in your classpath or use the `require` method to load the JAR file from your Ruby application. JRuby integrates nicely with the `org.eclipse.swt.Shell` and `org.eclipse.swf.widgets.Display` classes and is able to access all the UI widgets in the library. The code in Example 5-19 demonstrates how to handle button events in an SWT application.

Example 5-19. Simple JRuby SWT application

```
include Java
require 'swt'

import org.eclipse.swt.SWT
import org.eclipse.swt.layout.RowLayout
import org.eclipse.swt.widgets.Listener

d = org.eclipse.swt.widgets.Display.new
s = org.eclipse.swt.widgets.Shell.new(d)
but = org.eclipse.swt.widgets.Button.new(s, SWT::PUSH)
but.text = "Search"
```

```
l = org.eclipse.swt.widgets.Label.new(s,SWT::NONE)
l.text = "Click to Search"
l.set_size(100,75)

but.addListener(SWT::Selection, Listener.impl do |method, evt|
     l.text = 'searching...'
end)

s.layout = RowLayout.new
s.set_size(300,200)
s.open

while(!s.is_disposed) do d.sleep if(!d.read_and_dispatch) end
d.dispose
```

Discussion

The Glimmer project is a JRuby DSL for creating SWT applications using a declarative syntax. It was created by Andy Maleh and is an official Eclipse project. Install the Glimmer gem with this command:

```
$ jruby -S gem install glimmer
```

The gem provides a custom DSL for composing SWT applications. It has a declarative style, using keywords and accompanying blocks to define containers as well as individual components. The widget's models and event handlers can be associated to Ruby methods for custom event processing and state changes. You can see an example of the Glimmer DSL in Example 5-20.

Example 5-20. Writing an SWT application with Glimmer

```
include Java
require File.dirname(__FILE__) + "/../src/swt"

include Glimmer
import 'org.eclipse.swt.layout.GridLayout'

def user_name
    "default text"
end

def enabled
    true
end

@shell = shell {
  text "SWT"
  composite {
    layout GridLayout.new(2, false) #two columns with differing widths
    label { text "Hello World!"}
    text {
```

```
        text bind(self, :user_name)
        enabled bind(self, :enabled)
      }
    }
  }
}
@shell.open
```

See Also

- Recipe 5.10, "Accessing the System Tray"
- Recipe 5.11, "Swing Development with JRuby Domain-Specific Languages"
- SWT website, *http://www.eclipse.org/swt/*
- Glimmer website, *http://rubyforge.org/projects/glimmer/*

5.9 Accessing the Native Desktop

Problem

You want to create or communicate with a native application.

Solution

You can access a limited set of commonly used features in the native desktop through the `java.awt.Desktop` class introduced in Java 6. The `Desktop` class does not provide access to the entire desktop, but does allow you to perform common desktop activities such as opening the default browser, launching the default mail client, as well as printing or opening a file with its default application (Example 5-21).

Example 5-21. Java Desktop API

```
include Java
import java.awt.Desktop
import java.net.URI
import java.io.File

d = Desktop::desktop

# Open the browser
d.browse(URI.new("http://www.ora.com/")) if d.isSupported(Desktop::Action::BROWSE)

# Open your mail client and compose a message
d.mail(URI.new("mailto:jruby@ora.com")) if d.isSupported(Desktop::Action::MAIL)

# Launch the default jpg viewing application
d.open(File.new("conference_pic_1.jpg")) if d.isSupported(Desktop::Action::OPEN)

# Print a document
d.print(File.new("directions.twxt")) if d.isSupported(Desktop::Action::PRINT)
```

5.10 Accessing the System Tray

Problem

You want to use JRuby to create an application that runs in the Mac OS X, Windows, or KDE system tray.

Solution

Swing

You can access the Windows or Linux system tray through the Java `java.awt.System Tray` class, added in Java 6, as in Example 5-22.

Example 5-22. A Java system tray application

```
include Java

import java.awt.TrayIcon
import java.awt.event.MouseListener

if (java.awt.SystemTray::isSupported())

   tray = java.awt.SystemTray::system_tray
   image = java.awt.Toolkit::default_toolkit.get_image("tray.gif")

   popup = java.awt.PopupMenu.new
   exititem = java.awt.MenuItem.new("Exit")
   exititem.addActionListener {java.lang.System::exit(0)}

   oraitem = java.awt.MenuItem.new("Go To ORA")
   oraitem.addActionListener do
    java.awt.Desktop::desktop.browse(java.net.URI.new("http://www.ora.com"))
   end

   popup.add(exititem)
   popup.add(oraitem)
   trayIcon = TrayIcon.new(image, "Tray Demo", popup)
   trayIcon.image_auto_size = true

   trayIcon.addActionListener do |evt|
    trayIcon.displayMessage("Action","Tray Action!", \
      TrayIcon::MessageType::WARNING)
   end

   trayIcon.addMouseListener(MouseListener.impl do |method, evt|
       puts "mouse event #{method.to_s}"
   end

   tray.add(trayIcon)
end
```

SWT

The SWT library also includes a class for accessing the system tray:
`org.eclipse.swt.widgets.Tray` (Example 5-23). This SWT widget has the advantage of
being available on the Windows, Linux, and Mac platforms. The OS X implementation
places an icon in the desktop's status area.

Example 5-23. SWT system tray application

```
include Java
require 'swt-debug'

import org.eclipse.swt.SWT
import org.eclipse.swt.widgets.Listener
import org.eclipse.swt.widgets.MenuItem

d = org.eclipse.swt.widgets.Display.new
s = org.eclipse.swt.widgets.Shell.new(d)
image = org.eclipse.swt.graphics.Image.new(d, "tray.gif")
tray = d.system_tray
item = org.eclipse.swt.widgets.TrayItem.new(tray, SWT::NONE)
item.tool_tip_text = "SWT TrayItem"

item.addListener(SWT::DefaultSelection, Listener.impl do |evt|
     puts("default selection")
end)

menu = org.eclipse.swt.widgets.Menu.new(s, SWT::POP_UP)
menuitem = MenuItem.new(menu, SWT::PUSH)
menuitem.text = "Exit"

menuitem.addListener(SWT::Selection, Listener.impl do |method, evt|
     s.close
end)

item.addListener(SWT::MenuDetect, Listener.impl do |method, evt|
     menu.visible = true
end)

item.image = image
# exclude these parameters to hide the main window
#s.setBounds(10, 10, 100,100)
#s.open()
while(!s.is_disposed) do d.sleep if(!d.read_and_dispatch) end
image.dispose
d.dispose
```

See Also

- Recipe 5.8, "Creating SWT Applications"

5.11 Swing Development with JRuby Domain-Specific Languages

Problem

The trend toward declarative GUI design can be seen in the growth of web applications and the transition of established technologies to declarative models such as Adobe Flex and JavaFX Script. You want to use a JRuby-based DSL to develop your Swing applications.

Solution

There are a several different projects that present DSLs for creating Swing user interfaces.

Swiby

The Swiby project is a JRuby adaptation of the declarative GUI building portion of the JavaFX Script language. Install the Swiby gem:

```
$ jruby -S gem install swiby
```

Swiby's syntax and design is inspired from JavaFX Script, in which blocks are used to represent hierarchies of user interface containers and components. Properties are defined by single-line name-value declarations. The Swing and AWT class names are mapped to shorter, more concise names used in the DSL. Swiby eliminates some of JavaFX Script's capitalization when defining widgets and trailing colons after property declarations. Example 5-24 shows Swiby in action.

Example 5-24. Simple Swiby application

```
require 'rubygems'
require 'swiby'
require 'swiby/form'

class LabelModel
  attr_accessor :text
end
model = LabelModel.new
model.text = "Click to Search"

f = frame {
  title "Swiby Example"
  width 300
  height 100

  content {
  panel :layout => :flow do
    button("Search") { model.text="Searching...."}
    label {label bind(model, :text)}
```

```
    end
  }
}
f.visible = true
```

The Swiby project has some features that aren't found in JavaFX Script, like the ability to define your styles in an external file. The styles can be loaded and applied with the simple `use_styles` declaration. Example 5-25 shows how to alter the font by creating and loading a file named *styles.rb*.

Example 5-25. Defining Swiby styles

swibyapp.rb

```
frame {
  title "Swiby Example"
  width 300
  height 74
  use_styles "styles.rb"
  .
  .
```

styles.rb

```
create_styles {
  label(
    :font_family => Styles::VERDANA,
    :font_style => :italic,
    :font_size => 14,
    :color => 0xAA0000
  )
}
```

The gem also provides a useful form-building DSL. This is geared toward forms with simpler, grid-based layouts.

Cheri::Swing

The Cheri project is a framework that facilitates the creation of DSLs that implement the Builder pattern to create a hierarchy of objects. Cheri::Swing is one of these DSLs. Begin by installing the Cheri gem:

```
$ jruby -S gem install cheri
```

Its declarative syntax is very similar to Swiby and also provides access to Swing components as well as the AWT's image and geometry packages. Example 5-26 presents a Cheri application.

Example 5-26. Simple Cheri::Swing application

```
require 'rubygems'
require 'cheri/swing'
include Cheri::Swing
```

```
swing[:auto=>true]

f = frame('Cheri App') { |myframe|
  size 250,100

  flow_layout
  on_window_closing {|event| f.dispose}
  button('Search') {
    on_click {@l.set_text "Searching..."}
  }
  separator
  @l = label('Click to search')
}
f.visible = true
```

Setting the swing[:auto=>true] option allows you to eliminate the swing prefix in the component declaration: swing.frame becomes frame, etc.

Profligacy

The Profligacy library was created by Zed Shaw and takes a different approach than Cheri and Swiby, as we'll see shortly. First, install the Profligacy gem:

```
$ jruby -S gem install profligacy
```

Profligacy provides a custom DSL that includes a variety of time-saving syntactical improvements, as shown in Example 5-27.

Example 5-27. Profligacy search demo

```
require 'rubygems'
require 'profligacy/swing'

class SearchDemo
    include_package 'javax.swing'
    include_package 'java.awt'
    include Profligacy

    def initialize
      @ui = Swing::Build.new JFrame, :search, :lab do |c,i|
        c.search = JButton.new "Search"
        c.lab = JLabel.new "Click to Search"
        i.search = { :action => proc {|t,e| c.lab.text = "Searching..." } }
      end

      @ui.layout = FlowLayout.new
      @ui.build("Layout").default_close_operation = JFrame::EXIT_ON_CLOSE
    end
end

SwingUtilities.invoke_later lambda { SearchDemo.new }
```

Profligacy uses a custom layout language named LEL where you create something that resembles ASCII art to create a layout with named component spaces (Example 5-28).

Example 5-28. Profligacy LEL demo

```
require 'rubygems'
require 'profligacy/swing'
require 'profligacy/lel'

class LelSearchTest
  include_package 'javax.swing'
  include Profligacy

  layout = "
    [ search | _  ]
    [   _    | lab]
  "

  ui = Swing::LEL.new(JFrame,layout) do |c,i|
    c.search = JButton.new "Search"
    c.lab = JLabel.new "Click To Search"
    i.search= { :action => proc {|t,e| c.lab.text = "Searching..." } }
  end
  ui.build(:args => "LEL Search Example")
end
```

The brackets represent individual rows and the pipes character is a column delimiter.
Figure 5-1 shows the output after executing Example 5-28.

Figure 5-1. LEL Search Demo user interface

See Also

- Cheri website, *http://cheri.rubyforge.org/*
- Swiby website, *http://swiby.codehaus.org/*
- Profligacy website, *http://ihate.rubyforge.org/profligacy/*

5.12 Using the Monkeybars Framework for Swing Development

Problem

You want to develop a Swing application while following the model-view-controller (MVC) pattern.

Solution

Use Monkeybars, a library created by David Koontz, the author of Rawr. It uses the MVC design pattern, similar to web frameworks like Rails or Struts, to create JRuby client applications. Start by installing the Monkeybars gem:

```
$ jruby -S gem install monkeybars
```

The gem will add the Monkeybars tool to your JRuby execution path. This is similar to the *rails* command used by Ruby on Rails developers. Running *monkeybars* creates the main project folder and the project skeleton:

```
$ jruby -S monkeybars search_demo
```

Example 5-29 includes a Java class that we will use with Monkeybars. This class extends JFrame and contains a button with some accompanying text. The file should be located in the *src*.

Example 5-29. Java GUI class for use with Monkeybars

```java
import javax.swing.*;

public class SearchDemoJava extends JFrame {
    private JLabel message = new JLabel("Click to search");
    private JButton search = new JButton("Search");

    public SearchDemoJava(){
        this.setLayout(new java.awt.FlowLayout());
        this.setSize(300,100);
        add(search);
        add(message);
    }
}
```

The event-handling code and model data is defined in Ruby code. The **generate** Rake task, which was added along with the Monkeybars JAR file and several Ruby classes when the project was generated, is used to create the new model, view, and controller classes. Use the ALL parameter to create all these at once:

```
$ cd search_demo
$ jruby -S rake generate ALL="src/search"
(in C:/projects/search_demo)
Generating controller SearchController in file search_controller.rb
Generating model SearchModel in file search_model.rb
Generating view SearchView in file search_view.rb
```

The model class uses an instance variable to store messages that are displayed in the text label (Example 5-30). The variable is later mapped to a GUI component in the complementing view file.

Example 5-30. Monkeybars model file

```ruby
class SearchModel
    attr_accessor :search_message
```

```
    def initialize
         @search_message = "Starting"
    end
end
```

Open the *search_view.rb* file and assign the `SearchDemoJava` class as your view's display component by calling the `set_java_class` method. Use the `map` method to bind the model's instance variable to the text property of the label so that modifications to the model class will be reflected in the view component. The modified view class can be seen in Example 5-31.

Example 5-31. Monkeybars view class

```
class SearchView < ApplicationView
  set_java_class 'SearchDemoJava'
  map :model => :search_message, :view => "message.text"
end
```

The controller class is responsible for defining the view and model objects, event-handling, and managing the state of the application. Open *search_controller.rb* and you will see that the generator has already defined the view and model classes. It is still necessary to add the event-handling function for the search button. The search controller intercepts events from the view and directs them to a function that incorporates the instance variable name of the source, `search`, and the lowercase form of the event's Java type, `action_performed`. This is another inspiration from Rails and convention over configuration design. Example 5-32 shows the modified controller class.

Example 5-32. Monkeybars controller class

```
class SearchController < ApplicationController
  set_model 'SearchModel'
  set_view 'SearchView'
  set_close_action :exit

  def search_action_performed
      model.search_message = "Searching..."
      update_view
  end
end
```

Note that the new text value is set in Ruby model and not in the Java component. The `update_view` method redraws the GUI components, which then reevaluate the view mapping and display the new message.

Install the Rawr gem and run the `rawr install` command in your project's root directory. Edit the *src/main.rb* file and add a hook into your application by creating an instance of the controller class (Example 5-33).

Example 5-33. Monkeybars main execution file

```
begin
  # Your app logic here, i.e. YourController.instance.open
```

```
    require 'search_demo/search_controller'
    SearchController.instance.open
rescue Exception => e
```

Download or build a copy of *jruby-complete.jar* and place the file in the *lib/java* directory. Bundle the application as an executable JAR by calling the `rawr:jar` Rake task from the project's root directory:

```
$ jruby -S rake rawr:jar
```

By default, this produces a JAR file in the *package/deploy* directory. You can modify the name of the final JAR file by editing Rawr's *build_configiruation.yaml* file. Test the new application by running the JAR:

```
$ java -jar package/deploy/change_me.jar
```

Discussion

Example 5-31 showed the use of a UI component defined in Java, but you may want to use JRuby or a framework to generate the user interface. The class defined in Example 5-34 is fundamentally the same as that from Example 5-29.

Example 5-34. UI component defined in JRuby

```
include Java

class SearchDemoRuby  < javax.swing.JFrame
    attr_accessor :search, :message
    def initialize
      super
      self.layout = java.awt.FlowLayout.new
      add(@search = javax.swing.JButton.new("search"))
      add(@message = javax.swing.JLabel.new("Click to Search"))
      self.set_size(300,100)
    end
end
```

This example really demonstrates how the loose coupling between the components makes the view layer easily interchangeable. The view file is the only file in the MVC portion of the app that will need to be modified. Monkeybars support for Ruby-defined components is a little less elegant than the Java support but is expected to improve in the future. Remove the old **set_java_class** declaration and assign a new instance of the Ruby GUI class to the **@main_view_component** variable. This is shown in Example 5-35. Be sure to call the parent's constructor when overriding the view's default constructor.

Example 5-35. Monkeybars view class that uses a JRuby UI component

```
class SearchView < ApplicationView
# set_java_class "SearchDemoJava"
  def initialize
      super
      @main_view_component = SearchDemo.new
  end
```

```
def search
    @main_view_component.search
end
def message
    @main_view_component.message
end
map :model => :search_message, :view => "message.text"
end
```

In addition, you need to edit the *main.rb* file in order to have it load the JRuby GUI class:

```
begin
  # Your app logic here, i.e. YourController.instance.open
    require 'search_demo_ruby'
    require 'search_demo/search_controller'
    SearchController.instance.open
rescue Exception => e
```

Once this is in place, you can generate a new executable JAR file with Rawr and test your application.

See Also

- Monkeybars home page, *http://monkeybars.rubyforge.org/*
- Recipe 5.4, "Packaging Standalone Applications"

5.13 Creating Qt Applications with JRuby

Problem

You would like to use JRuby to build applications using the Qt GUI framework. Qt is a popular cross-platform application framework for creating user interfaces. It has a rich set of components such as the Web Browser and System Tray widgets.

Solution

The Qt Jambi project lets developers leverage the Qt framework through Java. Qt Jambi is available for download from *http://trolltech.com/downloads/*. Download the platform-specific bundle and add the files *qtjambi-version.jar* and *qtjambi-platform-version.jar* to your classpath.

Qt::JRuby is a library that brings several nice integration features when working directly with the Qt Jambi library from JRuby including a DSL for Qt. To use Qt::JRuby, you need to build the library from source. First, get the latest version of Qt::JRuby from its Git repository. Then, use Rake to build *qtjruby-core.jar* and install the wrapper RubyGem:

```
$ git clone git://github.com/nmerouze/qtjruby.git
Initialize qtjruby/.git
Initialized empty Git repository in /home/henry/qtjruby/.git/
```

```
remote: Counting objects: 391, done.
remote: Compressing objects: 100% (182/182), done.
Receiving objects: 100% (391/391), 59.30 KiB | 78 KiB/s, done.
Resolving deltas: 100% (180/180), done.
$ cd qtjruby/qtjruby-core
$ jruby -S rake
(in /home/henry/qtjruby/qtjruby-core)
ant -lib /opt/jruby-1.1.2/bin/../lib
Buildfile: build.xml

qtjruby-core:
    [javac] Compiling 14 source files to C:\home\devel\qtjruby\qtjruby-core\build
    [javac] Note: Some input files use unchecked or unsafe operations.
    [javac] Note: Recompile with -Xlint:unchecked for details.
    [jar] Building jar: C:\home\devel\qtjruby\qtjruby-core\lib\qtjruby-core.ja
r

BUILD SUCCESSFUL
Total time: 1 second
WARNING:  no rubyforge_project specified
WARNING:  RDoc will not be generated (has_rdoc == false)
  Successfully built RubyGem
  Name: qtjruby-core
  Version: 0.2.0
  File: qtjruby-core-0.2.0.gem
 /opt/jruby-1.1.2/bin/../bin/jruby -S gem install pkg/qtjruby-core-0.2.0.gem
Successfully installed qtjruby-core-0.2.0
1 gem installed
```

The Qt::JRuby library includes a Ruby module named `Qt` that allows you to reference the Qt Jambi classes without a package name or the `Q` prefix. For example, the class `com.trolltech.qt.gui.QPushButton` can simply be referred to as `Qt::PushButton`. This is an admittedly small detail, but one that makes code clearer and more readable. The library also maps Qt signals into blocks, similar to a technique used with JRuby Swing event handlers. Example 5-36 contains a basic Qt::JRuby application.

Example 5-36. Qt::JRuby application

```
Qt::Application.initialize(ARGV)
window = Qt::Widget.new
window.resize(300, 200)
l = Qt::HBoxLayout.new
window.window_title = 'QTJRuby Example'
window.layout = l

quit = Qt::PushButton.new("Search", window)
quit.font = Qt::Font.new("Times", 14, Qt::Font::Weight::Bold.value)

searchlab = Qt::Label.new("Click to Search", window)
quit.clicked { searchlab.text = "Searching..."    }

l.add_widget quit
l.add_widget searchlab
```

```
window.show
Qt::Application.exec
```

Start the application with this command:

```
$ jruby -S qtjruby qt_search_demo.rb
```

Discussion

You can also avoid the call to `qtjruby` by including its contents, a reference to the *qtjruby-core.jar* file and gem-loading logic, in your application. This may be useful when packaging your code as a redistributable application:

```
require 'qtjruby-core'

gem_path = Qt::JRuby.root / 'gems'
if File.exist? gem_path
  Gem.clear_paths
  Gem.path.unshift(gem_path)
end

Qt::Application.initialize(ARGV)
window = Qt::Widget.new
...
```

This example can now be run directly:

```
$ jruby qt_search_demo.rb
```

There is a DSL for Qt JRuby currently under development. It's pretty experimental and the API may change with the early releases. Start by building and installing the `qtjruby-dsl` gem:

```
$ cd qtjruby/qtjruby-dsl
$ jruby -S rake
```

The browser widget example that is distributed with Qt::JRuby nicely demonstrates the capabilities of the DSL (Example 5-37). Again, the component names are shortened and blocks are used to represent container relationships and service events.

Example 5-37. Qt::JRuby experimental DSL

```
require 'rubygems'
require 'qtjruby-dsl'

Qt.app do
  window :id => 'main' do
    create :browser_win, :type => :browser
    create :le_address, :type => :line_edit

    hbox do
      le_address
      button('Go').clicked do
        browser_win.load le_address.text
      end
    end
```

```
    browser_win.load 'http://www.ora.com'
  end
end
```

See Also

- Qt Jambi website, *http://trolltech.com/products/qt/features/language-support/java*
- Qt::JRuby blog, *http://qtjruby.org/blog*
- Git website, *http://git.or.cz/*

## CHAPTER 6

Build Tools

6.0 Introduction

Just about every software project, regardless of language or scope, needs to be *built* in some way. The build process can include steps including compiling code, running automated tests, file processing, packaging, and deployment, among others. Because there is significant commonality among build processes, a variety of specialized *build systems* are available. These systems allow you to describe your build process as a series of interdependent, reusable tasks. Ant, for example, allows you to replace this:

```
$ javac *.java
$ jar -cf my.jar *.class
```

With this:

```
$ ant jar
```

Or even (if `jar` is the default target):

```
$ ant
```

This chapter discusses techniques for building Java-based projects. In this context, Ruby can be used as the core of the build process or to enhance an existing build process. There are two major build systems used for Java projects: Ant and Maven. Both of these are projects of the Apache Software Foundation and both have extension mechanisms that support JRuby. This is the focus of the first few recipes. The later recipes describe two different Ruby-based build systems designed for Java projects: Raven and Buildr. All four of these build systems have merit: which to use for a particular project is largely a matter of preference. Raven and Buildr are significantly newer than Ant and Maven and, as a result, the communities around them are smaller.

The chapter ends with two recipes about the Hudson continuous integration server. The first of these addresses how to build Ruby projects that use the Rake build system. The second looks at using Ruby to add additional scripting to your build process inside Hudson.

6.1 Adding Ruby Scripting to Ant Builds

Problem

You are using Apache Ant as a build system and need to add some logic to your build that isn't easily accomplished with Ant's XML syntax.

Solution

Add the appropriate JRuby dependencies to Ant's *lib* directory and use the `script` task to include Ruby code inside your Ant build file. Example 6-1 shows a very simple usage of this task.

Example 6-1. Hello World from JRuby inside Ant

```xml
<?xml version="1.0" encoding="UTF-8"?>
<project name="project" default="package">
    <target name="simple">
        <script language="ruby">
                print "Hello World!"
        </script>
    </target>
</project>
```

Discussion

This task can use either the Bean Scripting Framework (BSF) or the Java Scripting (JSR 223) libraries discussed in Chapter 3 and, as a result, supports many more scripting languages than just Ruby. To use this task, you must make the appropriate dependencies available to Ant. For BSF, these dependencies are *jruby.jar* and *bsf.jar*, both included in the JRuby distribution's *lib* directory. For Java Scripting, you need the *jruby.jar* file from the JRuby distribution and *jruby-engine.jar*, available from *https:// scripting.dev.java.net/*. Recipe 3.2 and Recipe 3.3 contain more information about these APIs. As mentioned in the Solution above, these JAR files can be placed in Ant's *lib* directory. Alternatively, the dependencies can be declared inside the Ant build file as seen in Example 6-2. This latter method requires slightly more configuration, as you need to set up the appropriate Ant properties—`jruby.home` and `jsr223.engines.home` in the case of Example 6-2. In this example, those properties are defined in a *build.properties* file in the user's home directory.

Example 6-2. Defining JRuby dependencies inside the Ant file

```xml
<?xml version="1.0" encoding="UTF-8"?>
<project name="project" default="package">

    <property file="${user.home}/build.properties" />
    <path id="jruby">
        <fileset file="${jruby.home}/lib/jruby.jar" />
        <fileset file="${jsr223.engines.home}/lib/jruby-engine.jar" />
    </path>
```

```
    <target name="simple">
        <script language="ruby" classpathref="jruby">
            print "Hello #{$project.getProperty('user.name')}"
        </script>
    </target>
</project>
```

Example 6-2 also shows that the Ant project object is available to Ruby code as a global variable named $project. In addition to the project, all Ant properties, references, and targets are also available. However, it is frequently the case, as in Example 6-2, that the Ant property name contains the period character. In these cases, you need to use the getProperty() method to retrieve the values of these properties. If the user's name was available through an Ant property named user_name, we could instead have written:

```
    print "Hello #{$user_name}"
```

Ant targets can be executed by calling their execute method. Example 6-3 shows the usage of Ruby code inside Ant in order to express a complex conditional. In this example, we want some additional deployment step to be performed only when the build is run in a Continuous Integration (CI) environment and when the CI server used is Hudson. These indicators are passed into the Ant build using properties, which are then used by the Ruby script.

Example 6-3. Calling an Ant target from Ruby

```
<?xml version="1.0" encoding="UTF-8"?>
<project name="project" default="package">

    <property name="src.dir" value="${basedir}/src" />
    <property name="output.dir" value="${basedir}/bin" />
    <property name="deploy.dir" value="${basedir}/deploy" />
    <property name="output.file" value="${output.dir}/package.zip" />

    <target name="init">
        <mkdir dir="${output.dir}" />
        <mkdir dir="${deploy.dir}" />
    </target>

    <target name="package" depends="init">
        <zip destfile="${output.file}">
            <fileset dir="${src.dir}" />
        </zip>
        <script language="ruby" classpathref="jruby">
            <![CDATA[
            if ($cibuild == "true") && ($ciserver == "Hudson") then
                $deploy.execute()
            end
            ]]>
        </script>
    </target>

    <target name="deploy">
```

```
        <echo>Deploying file ${output.file}</echo>
        <copy file="${output.file}" todir="${deploy.dir}"/>
    </target>

</project>
```

Your Ruby code can access other scripts or libraries. For example, the deployment step in Example 6-3 could be done directly from Ruby code using the `FileUtils` module from the Ruby Standard Library:

```
<![CDATA[
require 'fileutils'
if ($cibuild != true) && ($ciserver == 'Hudson') then
    puts "Deploying file #{$project.getProperty('output.file')}..."
    FileUtils.cp $project.getProperty("output.file"),
        $project.getProperty("deploy.dir")
end
]]>
```

For this to work, you have to set the `jruby.home` system properties. This can be done with the `ANT_OPTS` environment variable. On Windows, you would run:

```
set ANT_OPTS=-Djruby.home="%JRUBY_HOME%"
```

On Linux or Mac OS X, you would use:

```
export ANT_OPTS=-Djruby.home="$JRUBY_HOME"
```

One final option to note is that you are not limited to including your Ruby script inline inside the `script` task. The task supports an `src` attribute that can contain the path to a script to be executed. Using an inline script versus an external file is largely a matter of length—once you are including more than 10 lines of code inline, it's probably a good idea to extract the code into an external file. External script files can also be useful if you need to reuse the same block of code in multiple Ant build files.

6.2 Using Ruby in Ant Conditions

Problem

Your Ant build has some conditional execution that is best expressed with Ruby code.

Solution

Set up the Ant classpath as described in Recipe 6.1 and use the `scriptcondition` Ant condition element. This element is set up similar to the script task described in Recipe 6.1. The key distinction is that conditions are evaluated to produce a Boolean result. Typically, the condition has a default value and the content of the condition would override this as necessary. For example, the Ant fragment in Example 6-4 will set a property named `user_has_text_files` to `true` if the user has any text files in their home directory.

Example 6-4. Using scriptcondition

```
<target name="setup">
    <condition property="user_has_text_files">
        <scriptcondition language="ruby" value="false">
            cwd = Dir.pwd
            Dir.chdir $project.getProperty("user.home")
            $self.setValue(true) if Dir.glob("**/*.txt")
            Dir.chdir cwd
        </scriptcondition>
    </condition>
</target>
```

In Example 6-4, the default result of the condition is `false`. This result is overridden to `true` by using the `$self` variable, which represents the condition object itself. As with the script task discussed in Recipe 6.1, the `$project` variable is set to the Ant `Project` object and all Ant properties are available as variables in the Ruby script.

Discussion

Ant conditions can be combined with `and`, `or`, `not`, and `xor` condition elements. Example 6-5 shows the combination of the condition from Example 6-4 with one of Ant's built-in conditions, `os`. In this example, we ensure that the `user_has_text_files` property is only set on Windows systems.

Example 6-5. Combining scriptcondition with other Ant conditions

```
<target name="setup">
    <condition property="user_has_text_files">
        <and>
            <os family="windows"/>
            <scriptcondition language="ruby" value="false">
                puts "hello"
                cwd = Dir.pwd
                Dir.chdir $project.getProperty("user.home")
                $self.setValue(true) if Dir.glob("**/*.txt")
                Dir.chdir cwd
            </scriptcondition>
        </and>
    </condition>
</target>
```

Ant exhibits "short-circuiting" behavior in that the second (and third and fourth, etc.) conditions are only evaluated if necessary. For example, if the fragment in Example 6-5 was executed on a non-Windows system, the Ruby code would not actually be executed as the first condition (`<os family=windows"/>`) evaluated to `false`. This can be a useful thing to keep in mind, as some conditions take longer to evaluate than others.

6.3 Writing an Ant Task in Ruby

Problem

You want to execute a Ruby script in multiple Ant build files.

Solution

Use Ant's `scriptdef` task to create a new task definition that executes a Ruby script. The `scriptdef` task has a child element named `attribute`, which can be used to pass attributes into the task. Example 6-6 defines an Ant task named `start-webrick` that can be used to start up an instance of the WEBrick HTTP server given a specific port number and document root.

Example 6-6. Using scriptdef to define a new Ant task

```
<?xml version="1.0" encoding="UTF-8"?>
<project name="project" default="start">

    <scriptdef name="start-webrick" language="ruby">
        <attribute name="port"/>
        <attribute name="root"/>
        <![CDATA[
            require 'webrick'
            include WEBrick

            server = HTTPServer.new(:Port => $attributes.get('port').to_i)
            server.mount("/", HTTPServlet::FileHandler, $attributes.get('root'))
            server.start
        ]]>
    </scriptdef>

    <target name="start">
            <start-webrick port="8000" root="${basedir}/files"/>
    </target>

</project>
```

6.4 Adding Ruby Scripting to Maven Builds

Problem

You are using Apache Maven as a build system and need to quickly add some additional steps to your build process.

Solution

Configure the JRuby Maven plugin in your Maven project definition file, *pom.xml*. Example 6-7 shows the use of this plugin. In this example, the plugin's `run` goal, which executes a Ruby script, is bound to the `process-resources` phase. This means that the inline Ruby script will be run before any compilation or tests occur.

Example 6-7. Using the JRuby Maven plugin

```xml
<project>
    <modelVersion>4.0.0</modelVersion>
    <groupId>org.jrubycookbook</groupId>
    <artifactId>maven-sample</artifactId>
    <packaging>pom</packaging>
    <version>1.0-SNAPSHOT</version>

    <build>
        <plugins>
            <plugin>
                <groupId>org.codehaus.mojo</groupId>
                <artifactId>jruby-maven-plugin</artifactId>
                <executions>
                    <execution>
                        <phase>generate-resources</phase>
                        <goals>
                            <goal>run</goal>
                        </goals>
                        <configuration>
                            <ruby>
                                require 'fileutils'
                                FileUtils.touch 'target/timestamp'
                            </ruby>
                        </configuration>
                    </execution>
                </executions>
                <!-- These are necessary due to an issue with
                    JRuby's Maven distribution. -->
                <dependencies>
                    <dependency>
                        <groupId>backport-util-concurrent</groupId>
                        <artifactId>backport-util-concurrent</artifactId>
                        <version>3.0</version>
                    </dependency>
                    <dependency>
                        <groupId>asm</groupId>
                        <artifactId>asm-all</artifactId>
                        <version>2.2.3</version>
                    </dependency>
                </dependencies>
            </plugin>
        </plugins>
    </build>
</project>
```

Discussion

It's also possible to execute a script from a file by using the `script` configuration element instead of `ruby`:

```
<configuration>
    <script>src/main/scripts/touch_timestamp.rb</script>
</configuration>
```

As with Ant's JRuby support, this plugin uses the `jruby.home` system property to set up the Ruby load path. And just as Ant supports an `ANT_OPTS` environment variable to pass system properties, Maven supports an environment variable named `MAVEN_OPTS`. On Windows, you would run:

```
set MAVEN_OPTS=-Djruby.home="%JRUBY_HOME%"
```

On Linux or Mac OS X, you would use:

```
export MAVEN_OPTS=-Djruby.home="$JRUBY_HOME"
```

The default load path for scripts executed inside the Maven plugin will be these paths, relative to the `jruby.home` system property:

- `lib/ruby/site_ruby/1.8`
- `lib/ruby/site_ruby`
- `lib/ruby/1.8`
- `lib/ruby/1.8/java`

It is possible to add additional entries to this list using the `libraryPaths` configuration element:

```
<configuration>
    <script>src/main/scripts/touch_timestamp.rb</script>
    <libraryPaths>
        <libraryPath>${user.home}/ruby/lib</libraryPath>
    </libraryPaths>
</configuration>
```

One downside to this plugin is that the released version of this plugin at the time of writing (1.0-beta-4) is written with an older version of JRuby, version 0.9.9. You should check the plugin's website for the latest version.

See Also

- JRuby Maven plugin website, *http://mojo.codehaus.org/jruby-maven-plugin/*
- Apache Maven website, *http://maven.apache.org/*

6.5 Writing a Maven Plugin with JRuby

Problem

You are using Apache Maven as a build system and want to reuse some Ruby script across different projects. A good example of this is to use the RedCloth Ruby library for generating project documentation using the Textile markup language.

Solution

Create a new Maven plugin project and add the dependencies discussed in Recipe 6.4 to both the project and the `maven-plugin-plugin` plugin. Example 6-8 contains a simple *pom.xml* project descriptor.

Example 6-8. Maven pom.xml file for a JRuby-based Maven plugin

```
<project>
    <modelVersion>4.0.0</modelVersion>
    <groupId>org.jrubycookbook</groupId>
    <artifactId>maven-textile-plugin</artifactId>
    <packaging>maven-plugin</packaging>
    <version>1.0-SNAPSHOT</version>
    <name>Maven Textile Plugin</name>
    <description>
        Generates site documentation from Textile sources using
        RedCloth.
    </description>
    <dependencies>
        <dependency>
            <groupId>org.codehaus.mojo</groupId>
            <artifactId>jruby-maven-plugin</artifactId>
            <version>1.0-beta-4</version>
        </dependency>
        <dependency>
            <groupId>backport-util-concurrent</groupId>
            <artifactId>backport-util-concurrent</artifactId>
            <version>3.0</version>
        </dependency>
        <dependency>
            <groupId>asm</groupId>
            <artifactId>asm-all</artifactId>
            <version>2.2.3</version>
        </dependency>
    </dependencies>
    <build>
        <plugins>
            <plugin>
                <artifactId>maven-plugin-plugin</artifactId>
                <dependencies>
                    <dependency>
                        <groupId>org.codehaus.mojo</groupId>
                        <artifactId>jruby-maven-plugin</artifactId>
                        <version>1.0-beta-4</version>
```

```
            </dependency>
            <dependency>
                <groupId>backport-util-concurrent</groupId>
                <artifactId>
                    backport-util-concurrent
                </artifactId>
                <version>3.0</version>
            </dependency>
            <dependency>
                <groupId>asm</groupId>
                <artifactId>asm-all</artifactId>
                <version>2.2.3</version>
            </dependency>
        </dependencies>
      </plugin>
    </plugins>
  </build>
</project>
```

Install the RedCloth RubyGem:

```
$ gem install RedCloth
```

Then create a Ruby class in the *src/main/scripts* directory that extends the `Mojo` class provided by the `jruby-maven-plugin` plugin. As with Maven plugins written in Java, the class is annotated with a goal name. Also similar to Java-based plugins, the plugin can be parameterized. Since Ruby is dynamically typed, it is necessary to explicitly define the parameter type using a type attribute of the parameter annotation. Once any parameters are defined, the plugin's execution logic goes in a method named `execute`. Example 6-9 defines a goal named `generate` that searches for Textile files and transforms them to HTML using RedCloth.

Example 6-9. Maven plugin written in Ruby

```ruby
include Java

require 'rubygems'
gem 'RedCloth'
require 'redcloth'

# Plugin that will transform all Textile-formatted files to HTML
# @goal "generate"
class GenerateMojo < Mojo

  # @parameter type="java.io.File" default-value="${basedir}/src/main/site/textile"
  def sourceDirectory;;end

  # @parameter type="java.io.File" default-value="${basedir}/target/site"
  def outputDirectory;;end

  def execute
      $outputDirectory.mkdirs

      Dir.chdir $sourceDirectory.absolutePath
```

```
    Dir.glob("*.tx") do |entry|
        info "Opening #{entry}"
        open(entry) { |f| @contents = f.read }
        r = RedCloth.new @contents
        # get the filename without extension
        short_name = entry.slice(0, entry.length - 3)
        out = java.io.File.new($outputDirectory, "#{short_name}.html").absolutePath
        info "Writing to #{out}"
        open(out, 'w') { |f|
            f.puts "<html><body>"
            f.puts r.to_html
            f.puts "</body></html>"
        }
    end

  end
end

run_mojo GenerateMojo
```

Discussion

In addition to the @goal annotation seen in Example 6-9, the JRuby Maven plugin supports all of the same class-level annotations as are supported for Java-based Maven plugins. You can use @phase to bind your plugin to a particular phase in Maven's build lifecycle, @requiresProject false to allow your plugin to be run without a Maven project, and so on. A complete list of annotations can be found on the Maven website. One feature that unfortunately does not work in the current release is automated plugin documentation. With Java-based plugins, Maven is able to use these same annotations to build documentation for each goal, but this does not yet work for JRuby-based plugins.

As with the examples in Recipe 6.4, it's necessary to set the jruby.home system property through the MAVEN_OPTS environment variable. If you are using a nondefault RubyGem installation location, it is also necessary to set the GEM_HOME environment variable.

Readers familiar with Maven plugins may note that the code in Example 6-9 is not a Maven report and will not actually be invoked as part of the Maven site generation process. Since Maven report plugins have some additional requirements around local-ization, adding the necessary code to achieve this is an exercise left to the reader.

See Also

- The Maven Plugin Developer Center, *http://maven.apache.org/plugin-developers/index.html*
- JRuby Maven Plugin website, *http://mojo.codehaus.org/jruby-maven-plugin/*

6.6 Building Java Projects with Raven

Problem

You need to build a Java project and wish to write your build script using Ruby rather than XML.

Solution

Use Raven, a build tool for Java project that is based on Ruby's Rake tool. Raven is essentially an add-on to Rake that provides Rake with additional Rake tasks to build Java projects. Raven is available as a RubyGem, so to install it simply run:

```
$ gem install raven
```

To use Raven, create a file named *Rakefile* in the root of your project and include all necessary tasks in this file. Example 6-10 contains the simplest of Raven build scripts.

Example 6-10. Simple Raven build script

```
require 'raven'

javac 'compile'
```

This script would be executed by running:

```
$ rake compile
```

Or:

```
$ jruby -S rake compile
```

This will compile all the Java files in a directory named *src/main/java*, following the Maven project convention (see upcoming sidebar). This default can be easily overridden, as seen in Example 6-11.

Example 6-11. Changing the default source directory

```
require 'raven'

javac 'compile' do |t|
    t.build_path << "src/java"
end
```

Discussion

Because Raven is based on Rake, any existing Rake task can be used within a Raven build. A good example of this is the **clean** task. Since Rake includes a clean task, Raven doesn't need to provide one, as seen in Example 6-12.

Example 6-12. Raven build with Rake tasks

```
require 'raven'
require 'rake/clean'

CLEAN.include('target')

javac 'compile'
```

Note that Raven actually doesn't require JRuby.

What's the Relationship Between Raven and Maven?

In short, not much. Raven is by no means a port of Maven to Ruby. If anything, it is much more closely related to Ant than Maven, especially in that Ant, Rake, and Raven all descend from make. Unlike Maven (or Buildr, which is discussed in Recipe 6.10), Raven is a *procedural* build system. The Rakefile describes a series of steps that need to be performed to build your project. Maven is (at least in part) a *declarative* build system where you provide metadata about your project and Maven determines the steps that need to be performed in order to build it.

Raven does follow Maven's directory naming conventions. By default, Java source files are expected to be in *src/main/java*, JUnit tests in *src/test/java*, compiled Java classes will be put into *target/classes*, etc.

Raven also has the ability to import a local Maven repository and wrap all of the JAR files in RubyGems. This can be done by running:

```
$ jruby -S raven import
```

See Also

- Raven project website, *http://raven.rubyforge.org/*
- Rake documentation, *http://docs.rubyrake.org/*

6.7 Referencing Libraries with Raven

Problem

You are using Raven to build your Java project and depend upon other libraries, such as those from Jakarta Commons.

Solution

Use the dependency Raven task to define a set of dependencies and then reference the set from the tasks that need the dependencies. Example 6-13 contains a Rakefile for a project that depends upon Jakarta Commons Logging and Jakarta Commons

HttpClient. The dependency on the HttpClient library is restricted to version 3.1 by using the `=>` operator.

Example 6-13. Rakefile with dependencies

```
1 require 'raven'
2
3 dependency 'compile_deps' do |t|
4     t.deps << ['commons-logging', {'commons-httpclient' => '3.1'}]
5 end
6
7 javac 'compile' => 'compile_deps'
8
9 javadoc 'jdoc' => 'compile_deps'
```

Discussion

When used in a task definition, as on lines 7 and 9 of Example 6-13, the `=>` operator establishes a dependency between tasks.

Raven uses the RubyGems packaging system to manage dependencies by wrapping JAR files into a RubyGem. In order to avoid, in the words of the Raven source code, polluting the regular local RubyGem repository, defined by the GEM_HOME environment variable, Raven stores its RubyGems in a *.raven* subdirectory of the user's home directory. As discussed in the sidebar within Recipe 6.6, it is possible to populate this directory with the contents of a local Maven repository by running:

```
raven import
```

The Raven team makes a public gem repository available at *http://gems.rubyraven .org/* that contains wrapped versions of all of the libraries in the central Maven repository (*http://repo1.maven.org/maven2/*). It is possible to set up your own private repository, as we'll see in the next recipe.

6.8 Hosting a Private Raven Repository

Problem

You are building a Java project with Raven and want to insulate your build process from any external network problems.

Solution

Create a private Raven repository by importing content from a Maven repository. This can be done with a few simple commands:

```
# Change /home/raven below to whatever directory you want to use.
$ mkdir /home/raven
$ cd /home/raven
```

```
$ raven repository
$ raven server
```

This will import all artifacts from the central Maven repository and then start a web server on port 2233. To reference this repository in your Rakefile, add this line after the require statements:

```
set_sources(["http://localhost:2233"])
```

Discussion

The repository command used above has a few interesting options. First, it is possible to restrict the import to a subset of the repository by passing a list of project identifiers to the command. For example, to import only Jakarta Commons HttpClient and JUnit, you would run:

```
$ raven repository commons-httpclient junit
```

It is also possible to import a different Maven repository using the -m option. For example, to import JBoss's Maven repository, run:

```
$ raven -m http://repository.jboss.com/maven2/ repository
```

6.9 Running JUnit Tests with Raven

Problem

You are building your Java project with Raven and want to execute some JUnit unit tests.

Solution

Place your unit tests in the *src/test/java* directory, create a **dependency** task for any test dependencies, and then use the **junit** Raven task as seen in Example 6-14. By default, Raven will search for classes whose names start with **Test**, but in Example 6-14, this default is overridden to include only those classes with names *ending* with **Test**.

Example 6-14. Unit testing with Raven

```
require 'raven'

dependency 'compile_deps' do |t|
    t.deps << ['commons-logging', {'commons-httpclient' => '3.1'}]
end

dependency 'test_deps' => 'compile_deps' do |t|
    t.deps << {'junit' => '3.8.2'}
end

javac 'compile' => 'compile_deps'

junit 'test' => ['compile', 'test_deps'] do |t|
```

```
        t.test_classes << "**/*Test.java"
    end
```

You will see the test results on the console. If the tests pass, you'll see an OK message:

```
$ rake test
(in /home/justin/raven-sample1)
...
Running test org.jrubycookbook.SomeTest
.
Time: 0

OK (1 test)
```

A test failure will include the stack trace:

```
$ rake test
(in /home/justin/raven-sample1)
...
Running test org.jrubycookbook.SomeTest
.F
Time: 0
There was 1 failure:
1) testTest(org.jrubycookbook.SomeTest)junit.framework.AssertionFailedError
        at org.jrubycookbook.SomeTest.testTest(SomeTest.java:8)
        at sun.reflect.NativeMethodAccessorImpl.invoke0(Native Method)
        at sun.reflect.NativeMethodAccessorImpl.invoke(NativeMethodAccessorImpl.
java:39)
        at sun.reflect.DelegatingMethodAccessorImpl.invoke(DelegatingMethodAcces
sorImpl.java:25)

FAILURES!!!
Tests run: 1,  Failures: 1,  Errors: 0

There were failures!
```

See Also

- JUnit website, *http://www.junit.org*

6.10 Building Java Projects with Buildr

Problem

You need to build a Java project and wish to define your project's build using Ruby rather than XML.

Solution

Use Buildr, a declarative build system for Java code written in Ruby. Buildr is available as a RubyGem; installation can be done by running:

```
$ gem install buildr
```

Buildr uses a file named *buildfile** to define a project. A minimal *buildfile* such as the one seen in Example 6-15 defines the project's name (line 11), the project's group (line 13), a description of the project (line 10), the current version of the project (line 12), and the packaging type of the project (line 14).

Example 6-15. Minimal Buildr buildfile

```
10 desc "The Chapter 6 buildr project"
11 define "ch06-buildr" do
12   project.version = "1.0"
13   project.group = "org.jrubycookbook"
14   package(:jar)
15 end
```

Based on this *buildfile*, Buildr will assume that this is a project containing Java sources in a directory named *src/main/java* and JUnit test cases in a directory named *src/test/ java*. The generated JAR file will be named *ch06-buildr-1.0.jar*. To build the project (which for Buildr means compiling the source code and running the tests), simply run:

```
$ buildr
```

To build the JAR file, run:

```
$ buildr package
```

These commands can be run in the project's root directory or any subdirectory.

Discussion

If you have an existing Java project, especially one that uses Maven as its build system, Buildr can automatically create this file for you. Run `buildr` from the project's root directory and select the appropriate option:

```
$ buildr
To use Buildr you need a buildfile. Do you want me to create one?:
1. From maven2 pom file
2. From directory structure
3. Skip
? 1
Created /home/edelsonj/kramer/buildfile
```

When creating a *buildfile* from an existing Maven project's *pom.xml* file, Buildr is able to extract all of the information seen in Example 6-15 as well as all of the project's dependencies. The importer can be a little over-enthusiastic when it comes to dependencies, so always check the resulting *buildfile*. If your Maven project includes submodules, the generated *buildfile* will include information about those submodules.

When creating a *buildfile* from a directory structure, Buildr will only determine the project's name (using the current directory name) and the packaging type. Example 6-16 contains a *buildfile* generated in this manner.

---

* Buildr will also search for a file named *Buildfile*.

Example 6-16. Generated buildfile

```
# Generated by Buildr 1.3.1.1, change to your liking
# Version number for this release
VERSION_NUMBER = "1.0.0"
# Version number for the next release
NEXT_VERSION = "1.0.1"
# Group identifier for your projects
GROUP = "buildr-temp"
COPYRIGHT = ""

# Specify Maven 2.0 remote repositories here, like this:
repositories.remote << "http://www.ibiblio.org/maven2/"

desc "The Buildr-test project"
define "buildr-test" do

  project.version = VERSION_NUMBER
  project.group = GROUP
  manifest["Implementation-Vendor"] = COPYRIGHT
  compile.with # Add classpath dependencies
  package(:jar)
end
```

Comparing Raven and Buildr

As discussed in Recipe 6.6, there is a substantial architectural difference between Raven and Buildr, which parallels the difference between Ant and Maven. Raven is a procedural build system—your *Rakefile* explicitly defines the tasks available to build your project. Buildr, on the other hand, is a declarative build system—your *buildfile* provides information about your project, which Buildr uses to determine how to build your project. Comparing Example 6-15 with some of the sample Raven build files from recipes earlier in this chapter illustrates this difference—every task in the Raven builds needs to be declared explicitly (even if those tasks are set up with intelligent defaults) whereas the minimal *buildfile* in Example 6-15 can be used to compile, run tests, produce javadoc, etc.

To see the full list of available Buildr tasks, run:

```
$ buildr help:tasks
```

See Also

- Buildr website, *http://incubator.apache.org/buildr/*

6.11 Referencing Libraries with Buildr

Problem

You are using Buildr to build your Java project and depend upon other libraries, such as those from Jakarta Commons.

Solution

Pass the list of dependencies to the `compile.with` method. Each dependency is defined by four attributes: group, name, packaging type, and version. For example, if your code depends upon Apache HttpClient and Jakarta Commons Logging, you would specify:

```
compile.with "org.apache.httpcomponents:httpclient:jar:4.0-alpha4",
  "org.apache.httpcomponents:httpcore:jar:4.0-beta1",
  "commons-logging:commons-logging:jar:1.1.1"
```

Buildr will look for dependencies in your local Maven repository (in the *.m2/ repository* subdirectory of your home directory). If it cannot find the dependencies there, it will attempt to download them from a remote repository. As a result, it is also necessary to add this line to your *buildfile*:

```
repositories.remote << "http://repo1.maven.org/maven2/"
```

Discussion

Buildr's dependency mechanism is entirely based upon the Maven repository structure. Unlike Raven, which uses a RubyGems-based dependency mechanism, any library in an existing Maven repository can be used as part of a Buildr build. This includes the libraries in the *central* repository (at *http://repo1.maven.org/maven2/*), as well as other public Maven repositories hosted by Sun (*http://download.java.net/maven/2/*) and JBoss (*http://repository.jboss.com/maven2/*), among others. Individual developers and software development organizations can also host private Maven repositories.

Although Buildr will sometimes correctly resolve dependencies transitively, this functionality does not always work. Expect support for transitive dependencies to improve in upcoming versions.

See Also

- Introduction to Maven Repositories, *http://maven.apache.org/guides/introduction/ introduction-to-repositories.html*

6.12 Building with Rake Inside Hudson

Problem

You want to build a software project that uses Rake as its build system in a continuous manner. This could be on a schedule (i.e., every day at noon) or upon every submission to a version control system like Subversion.

Solution

Use a continuous integration server that supports Rake, such as Hudson. Once the Hudson Rake plugin is installed, you can simply add a Rake execution to your job, as in Figure 6-1.

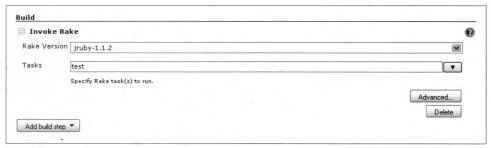

Figure 6-1. Rake build step in Hudson job configuration

Discussion

To install the Rake plugin in Hudson, use the Hudson Plugin Manager, which can be found under the Manage Hudson menu. Inside the Plugin Manager, select the Available tab to see the list of available plugins. Check the box next to the Rake plugin listing (Figure 6-2) and click the Install button. After the plugin has been installed, you will need to restart Hudson.

Figure 6-2. Rake plugin entry in the Plugin Manager

Hudson's Rake plugin allows you to configure multiple Ruby runtimes. This allows you to have some projects built against MRI and some projects built against JRuby within the same continuous integration server. This is done through the System Configuration screen, seen in Figure 6-3.

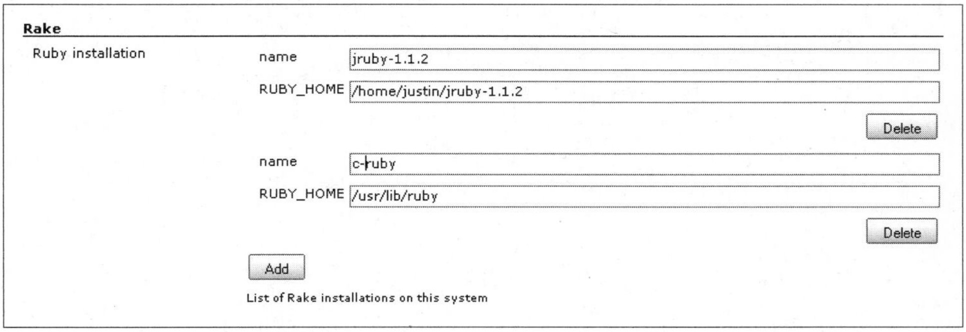

Figure 6-3. Multiple Ruby runtimes in Hudson

See Also

- Hudson website, *https://hudson.dev.java.net/*
- *http://hudson.gotdns.com/wiki/display/HUDSON/Rake+plugin*, Hudson Rake plugin

6.13 Adding Ruby Script to a Hudson Job

Problem

You have some additional build steps that need to be done as part of your build process when executed through the Hudson continuous integration server.

Solution

Use the Hudson Ruby plugin. This plugin allows you to add arbitrary Ruby script as a build step in your job. Figure 6-4 shows a job with two build steps. The first executes the Ant target named war and the second runs some Ruby code that copies all WAR files into a temporary directory.

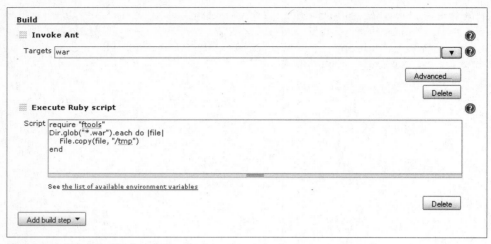

Figure 6-4. Using the Hudson Ruby plugin

Discussion

As with the Rake plugin discussed in Recipe 6.12, the Ruby plugin can be downloaded and installed through Hudson's Plugin Manager. Unlike the Rake plugin, the Ruby plugin does not support multiple runtimes. It will only execute the **ruby** command on your PATH. Thus, if want to use this plugin with JRuby, it will be necessary to create a copy (or symbolic link) of the *jruby* script included with the JRuby distribution named *ruby* and ensure that this script is on your PATH before any other Ruby. The plugin does make debugging simple by outputting the Ruby version number in the build's console output, like this:

```
[workspace] $ ruby -v /tmp/hudson35926.rb
ruby 1.8.5 (2007-09-24 patchlevel 114) [i386-linux]
```

Hudson makes a number of environment variables available to Ruby scripts executed in this manner. These include the name of the job (**JOB_NAME**), the build number (**BUILD_NUMBER**), and the Hudson URL (**HUDSON_URL**). A full listing is available through the Hudson web interface.

See Also

- *http://hudson.gotdns.com/wiki/display/HUDSON/Ruby+plugin*, Hudson Ruby plugin

## CHAPTER 7

Testing

7.0 Introduction

The focus of this chapter is the topic of automated testing, specifically, testing Java code with Ruby. There are several key advantages of using a dynamic language, such as Ruby, to test code written in a statically typed language, such as Java:

- Automated test cases tend to require a lot of bootstrapping code. Using a *domain-specific language* (DSL) such as those provided by the Ruby frameworks like dust and Expectations can cut down on this repetitive code.

- Dynamic languages make it very easy to create mock objects. JRuby, for example, allows you to directly instantiate Java interfaces.

- Open classes allow code to be modified at runtime to facilitate testing.

There are a variety of testing frameworks available in Ruby, the most popular of which are wrapped into a JRuby-based project called JtestR. JtestR is an open source project that Ola Bini and Anda Abramovici, developers at ThoughtWorks, started in 2008 with the purpose of making it easy to test Java code with a variety of Ruby testing frameworks. As of the current version 0.3, JtestR includes support for:

- Test/Unit
- RSpec
- Expectations
- dust
- Mocha

In addition, JtestR supports the Java testing frameworks JUnit and TestNG, making it a "one-stop shop" for testing frameworks.

JtestR is available for download from *http://jtestr.codehaus.org*.

7.1 Unit Testing Java Code with Test/Unit

Problem

You want to test your Java code using a more concise syntax than is available from Java testing frameworks such as JUnit and TestNG, but with a minimal learning curve for developers familiar with JUnit.

Solution

Use JtestR's support for the Ruby testing framework Test/Unit. Test/Unit uses similar semantics to JUnit:[*] test cases extend a specific test case class and test methods follow a naming convention. In the case of Test/Unit, test cases must extend `Test::Unit::Test Case` and test methods are prefixed with `test_`. Example 7-1 shows a simple Test/Unit class that tests the `size()` method of `java.util.ArrayList`.

Example 7-1. Simple Test/Unit

```
class TestArrayList < Test::Unit::TestCase

  def test_that_size_method_works
    list = java.util.ArrayList.new
    assert_equal(0, list.size)
    list << 'first'
    list << 'second'
    assert_equal(2, list.size)
  end

end
```

Discussion

Like JUnit, Test/Unit supports the use of a setup method (named `setup`) into which you can extract code that needs to be executed prior to each test. For example, if a second test method was added to Example 7-1, it would make sense to put the creation of the new `ArrayList` instance into this `setup` method, as seen in Example 7-2.

Example 7-2. Test/Unit class with setup method

```
class TestArrayList < Test::Unit::TestCase

  def setup
    @list = java.util.ArrayList.new
  end

  def test_that_size_method_works
    assert_equal(0, @list.size)
    @list << 'first'
```

---

[*] That is, JUnit prior to the addition of annotation support.

```
  @list << 'second'
  assert_equal(2, @list.size)
end

def test_that_empty_works
  assert(@list.empty)
  @list << 'first'
  @list << 'second'
  assert(!@list.empty)
end

end
```

Test/Unit also supports the use of a method named **teardown** for cleanup after each test is run.

Test/Unit tests can be run without any additional configuration with JtestR. Simply place the test class files in a directory named *test/unit* and start JtestR's command-line test runner. This class, along with all of JtestR's dependencies can be found in the JtestR JAR file, available from the JtestR website. You can run the JtestR command-line test runner with the command:

```
$ java -cp ~/jtestr-0.3.jar org.jtestr.JtestRRunner
```

To reduce the amount of typing necessary, you may want to add the JtestR JAR file to your classpath:

```
$ export CLASSPATH=~/jtestr-0.3.jar:$CLASSPATH
```

When you run JtestR with the default options, your test cases will be executed and you will see the results on the console:

```
$ java org.jtestr.JtestRRunner
Unit TestUnit: 2 tests, 0 failures, 0 errors
```

If the tests do not pass, you will see the test methods that are in failure. If **java.util.ArrayList** did not perform correctly, you would see something like the following:

```
Failure:
test_that_empty_works(TestArrayList)
...
<false> is not true.

Failure:
test_that_size_method_works(TestArrayList)
...
<2> expected but was
<3>.

Unit TestUnit: 2 tests, 2 failures, 0 errors

Exception in thread "main" java.lang.RuntimeException: Tests failed
        at org.jtestr.JtestRRunner.execute(JtestRRunner.java:117)
        at org.jtestr.JtestRRunner.main(JtestRRunner.java:163)
```

See Also

- Test/Unit documentation, *http://www.ruby-doc.org/stdlib/libdoc/test/unit/rdoc/*

7.2 Unit Testing Java Code with dust

Problem

You want to test your Java code using a more concise syntax than is available from Java testing frameworks such as JUnit and TestNG, and find Test/Unit to be too verbose.

Solution

Use Jay Fields's dust library, support for which is included with JtestR. dust provides an alternate syntax for writing tests that takes advantage of Ruby language features to create a domain-specific language (DSL) for testing. Example 7-3 contains the dust version of the tests in Example 7-2.

Example 7-3. Unit testing with dust

```
unit_tests do
    test "that size method works" do
        @list = java.util.ArrayList.new
        assert_equal(0, @list.size)
        @list << 'first'
        @list << 'second'
        assert_equal(2, @list.size)
    end

    test "that empty method works" do
        @list = java.util.ArrayList.new
        assert @list.empty
        @list << 'first'
        @list << 'second'
        assert !@list.empty
    end
end
```

As with Test/Unit tests, dust tests can be run through JtestR with no special configuration.

Discussion

Under the covers, dust converts the body of the block passed to the `unit_tests` method into a Ruby class in the `Units` module. The name is derived from the filename. If Example 7-3 was contained in a file named *lists_test.rb*, the generated class would be `Units::ListsTests`. Each call to the test method is converted to a method in this generated class. The name of the method is derived from the name given. The generated class for Example 7-3 includes methods named `test_that_size_method_works` and `test_that_empty_method_works`.

In addition to the `unit_tests` method seen in Example 7-3, dust also supports a `functional_tests` method. The only difference between the two methods is that tests defined within the `functional_tests` method are placed in a class in the `Functionals` module.

Under the default JtestR configuration, these generated class and method names are only seen when a test fails. For example:

```
Failure:
test_that_size_method_works(Units::ListTests)
...
<2> expected but was
<3>.
```

 Unlike Test/Unit, dust does not support **setup** or **teardown** methods.

See Also

- dust documentation, *http://dust.rubyforge.org*
- Jay Fields's introduction to dust, *http://blog.jayfields.com/2007/08/rubygems-dust .html*

7.3 Unit Testing Java Code with Expectations

Problem

You want to test your Java code using a more concise syntax than is available from Java testing frameworks such as JUnit and TestNG and want to ensure you follow some testing best practices, specifically limiting the number of assertions per test to one.

Solution

Use JtestR's support for the Expectations framework. Like dust, Expectations provides a domain-specific language (DSL) for writing tests. Unlike dust, Expectations does not use the standard Test/Unit assertion methods. Instead, each test makes an assertion about the return value of the test. Example 7-4 contains the same tests seen in prior recipes using Expectations.

Example 7-4. Unit testing with Expectations

```
Expectations do
    expect 0 do
        list = java.util.ArrayList.new
        list.size
    end

    expect 2 do
        list = java.util.ArrayList.new
        list << 'first'
        list << 'second'
        list.size
    end

    expect true do
        list = java.util.ArrayList.new
        list.empty
    end

    expect false do
        list = java.util.ArrayList.new
        list << 'first'
        list << 'second'
        list.empty
    end
end
```

JtestR's support for Expectations is not automatic; it must be enabled through configuration. To do so, first determine the naming convention you will use for Expectations-based tests. Then create a file named *jtestr_config.rb* in the *test* directory of your project. This file should contain a line such as the following:

```
expectation Dir["test/expectations/*.rb"]
```

In this case, we declare that any file in the *test/expectations* directory is meant to be run with Expectations. You could also use a filename-based naming convention:

```
expectation Dir["test/**/*_expect.rb"]
```

Or even declare individual files:

```
expectation Dir["test/unit/list_tests_expect.rb"]
```

Discussion

The output of Expectations is different than that for Test/Unit or dust tests, but the information conveyed is similar:

```
Expectations .F.F
Finished in 0.00206 seconds

Failure: 2 failed, 0 errors, 2 fulfilled

--Failures--
file </home/justin/list-tests/test/expectations/test.rb>
```

```
line <7>
expected: <3> got: <2>

file </home/justin/list-tests/test/expectations/test.rb>
line <19>
expected: <true> got: <false>
```

See Also

- Expectations documentation, *http://expectations.rubyforge.org*
- Jay Fields's introduction to Expectations, *http://blog.jayfields.com/2007/12/ruby -expectation-gem.html*

7.4 Testing Java Code with RSpec

Problem

You want to write behavior-orientated tests for your Java code.

Solution

Use JtestR's support for the RSpec Behavior-Driven Development (BDD) framework. RSpec is actually composed of two different frameworks for writing tests: the Spec framework and the Story framework.

Spec framework

RSpec Spec tests describe the behavior of an object through a series of assertions about the behavior of the object. These assertions are referred to as *examples*. The Spec file in Example 7-5 describes the behavior of the `java.util.HashSet` class.

Example 7-5. RSpec Spec file for java.util.HashSet

```
import java.util.HashSet

describe HashSet do
  before(:each) do
    @set = HashSet.new
  end

  it "should be empty" do
    @set.should be_empty
  end

  it "should be of size one after an item is added" do
    @set << "foo"
    @set.size.should == 1
  end

  it "should be of size one after an item is added twice" do
```

```
    @set << "foo"
    @set << "foo"
  @set.size.should == 1
end

it "should be of size two after two items are added" do
    @set << "foo"
    @set << "bar"
  @set.size.should == 2
end
end
```

By default, JtestR will execute files in any test directory whose filenames end with
spec.rb as an RSpec Spec file. If you place the file from Example 7-5 in the unit directory
and execute the command-line test runner, you will see output like this:

```
$ java org.jtestr.JtestRRunner
Unit Spec: 4 examples, 0 failures, 0 errors
```

Story framework

RSpec stories are generally composed of two files; one that describes the behavior of
an object in more-or-less plain text, referred to as the story, and another that translates
the behavior descriptions in the first file into method calls on the actual object, referred
to as the steps. For example, Example 7-6 contains a story that describes the behavior
of the `retains()` method of `java.util.ArrayList` and Example 7-7 contains the steps
corresponding to this story. These files are associated with the block at the end of the
steps file.

Example 7-6. Story about java.util.ArrayList

```
Story: retain the content of one ArrayList in another
  I want to retain only the contents of one ArrayList in another
  To create the union of the two lists

  Scenario: there is no overlap
      Given my ArrayList is a new ArrayList
      And my other ArrayList is a new ArrayList
    And my ArrayList contains "one"
    And my ArrayList contains "two"
    And my other ArrayList contains "three"
    When I retain only the contents of my other ArrayList to my ArrayList
    Then my ArrayList should be empty

  Scenario: there is some overlap
      Given my ArrayList is a new ArrayList
      And my other ArrayList is a new ArrayList
    And my ArrayList contains "one"
    And my ArrayList contains "two"
    And my ArrayList contains "three"
    And my other ArrayList contains "one"
    And my other ArrayList contains "two"
    When I retain only the contents of my other ArrayList to my ArrayList
```

```
        Then my ArrayList should have a size of 2
        And my ArrayList should contain "one"
        And my ArrayList should contain "two"
```

Example 7-7. Steps for java.util.ArrayList story

```
import java.util.ArrayList

$lists = { }

steps_for(:arraylist) do
  Given('my $list_name is a new ArrayList') do |list_name|
    $lists[list_name] = ArrayList.new
  end
  Given('my $list_name contains "$object"') do |list_name, object|
      $lists[list_name] << object
  end
  When('I retain only the contents of my $other_list_name to my $list_name') do
    |other_list_name,list_name|
      $lists[list_name].retain_all($lists[other_list_name])
  end
  Then('my $list_name should have a size of $size') do |list_name,size|
      $lists[list_name].size.should == size.to_i
  end
  Then('my $list_name should contain "$object"') do |list_name,object|
      $lists[list_name].contains(object).should == true
  end
  Then('my $list_name should be empty') do |list_name|
    $lists[list_name].should be_empty
  end
end

with_steps_for(:arraylist) do
  run 'test/stories/arraylist.story'
end
```

To run RSpec stories with JtestR, simply place the story and steps files in the *stories* subdirectory of the *test* directory. If you execute the command-line test runner, you will see output like this:

```
$ java org.jtestr.JtestRRunner
Stories: 2 scenarios, 0 failures, 0 errors
```

Discussion

Both the Spec and Story frameworks benefit from enabling verbose output. This can be done using command-line options (as described in Recipe 7.7) or by creating a *jtestr_config.rb* file in the *test* directory. For the former, simply place this line in the configuration file:

```
output_level :VERBOSE
```

For example, when running the Story and Spec in the examples in this recipe, the following is output:

```
$ java org.jtestr.JtestRRunner
should be empty(Java::JavaUtil::HashSet): .
should be of size one after an item is added(Java::JavaUtil::HashSet): .
should be of size one after an item is added twice(Java::JavaUtil::HashSet): .
should be of size two after two items are added(Java::JavaUtil::HashSet): .
Unit Spec: 4 examples, 0 failures, 0 errors

there is no overlap(retain the content of one ArrayList in another): .
there is some overlap(retain the content of one ArrayList in another): .
Stories: 2 scenarios, 0 failures, 0 errors
```

For the Spec framework, JtestR supports a variety of output formats. Most interesting is the HTML output, which allows you to create nice-looking reports. To enable this, add the following line to your *jtestr_config.rb* file:

```
rspec_formatter ["h", "spec_output.html"]
```

This will output the report to a file named *spec_output.html*. Figure 7-1 shows a sample of this output.

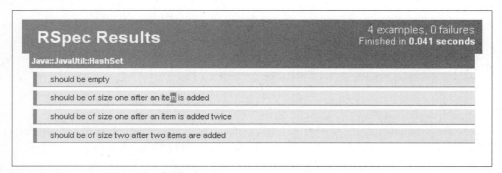

Figure 7-1. Positive RSpec HTML output

If one of the examples fails, then your output will illustrate that, as in Figure 7-2.

See Also

- RSpec website, *http://rspec.info*
- Introduction to BDD, *http://dannorth.net/introducing-bdd*
- Recipe 7.8, "Using the JtestR Command-Line Options"

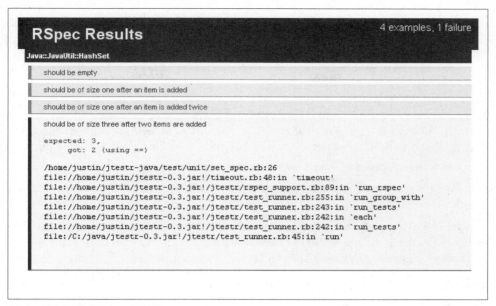

RSpec Results　　　　　　　　　　　　　　　　　　4 examples, 1 failure

Java::JavaUtil::HashSet

```
    should be empty

    should be of size one after an item is added

    should be of size one after an item is added twice

    should be of size three after two items are added

    expected: 3,
         got: 2 (using ==)

    /home/justin/jtestr-java/test/unit/set_spec.rb:26
    file://home/justin/jtestr-0.3.jar!/timeout.rb:48:in `timeout'
    file://home/justin/jtestr-0.3.jar!/jtestr/rspec_support.rb:89:in `run_rspec'
    file://home/justin/jtestr-0.3.jar!/jtestr/test_runner.rb:255:in `run_group_with'
    file://home/justin/jtestr-0.3.jar!/jtestr/test_runner.rb:243:in `run_tests'
    file://home/justin/jtestr-0.3.jar!/jtestr/test_runner.rb:242:in `each'
    file://home/justin/jtestr-0.3.jar!/jtestr/test_runner.rb:242:in `run_tests'
    file:/C:/java/jtestr-0.3.jar!/jtestr/test_runner.rb:45:in `run'
```

Figure 7-2. Failed RSpec HTML output

7.5 Creating Mock Objects with Mocha

Problem

You want to test a Java class that has dependencies on other classes and want to insulate your tests from changes in the behavior of those other classes.

Solution

Use Mocha, a Ruby mocking and stubbing framework that is included with JtestR. Mocha allows you to create instances of Java interfaces and classes that exhibit a specific behavior. Mock objects can be used in any type of test supported by JtestR. In Example 7-8, Mocha is used to create a mock instance of `java.util.Collection`, which is passed to an instance of `java.util.ArrayList`. This test validates the behavior of the `retainAll()` method, specifically that it calls the `contains()` method on the supplied `Collection` object the correct number of times.

Example 7-8. Unit test with dust and Mocha

```
unit_tests do
    test "that retainAll only calls contains" do
        list = java.util.ArrayList.new
        list << 'first'
        list << 'second'
        list << 'third'
```

```
        other = java.util.Collection.new
        other.expects(:contains).returns(true).times(3)

        list.retainAll(other)
    end
end
```

If another other method is called on the Collection object, an exception will be thrown and the test will fail. For example, if java.util.ArrayList implemented the retainsAll() method by iterating through the collection, this error would be output:

```
    #<Mock:0x4f4>.contains - expected calls: 1, actual calls: 0
```

Meaning that the mock expected the contains() method to be called, but that did not occur.

Mocha can also specify the set of parameters to expect. This feature can be used to enhance the test in Example 7-8 to test that ArrayList calls the contains() methods in the proper sequence. This new test can be seen in Example 7-9.

Example 7-9. Expecting a specific parameter

```
unit_tests do
    test "that retainAll calls contains once per item in the list" do
        list = java.util.ArrayList.new
        list << 'first'
        list << 'second'
        list << 'third'

        other = java.util.Collection.new
        other.expects(:contains).with('first').returns(true)
        other.expects(:contains).with('second').returns(true)
        other.expects(:contains).with('third').returns(true)

        list.retainAll(other)
    end
end
```

Discussion

Mocha can create mock objects for Java classes as well as interfaces. To mock a class, pass the class to the mock method. The only restriction on mocking concrete classes is that you cannot mock final classes or methods. For example, you cannot create a mock instance of java.lang.String like this:

```
    s = mock(java.lang.String)
    s.expect(:length).return(5)
```

By default, when you create a mock for concrete classes, none of the original behavior of the class is retained—any method that will be called needs to be defined through the expects method. This behavior can be altered by passing an array of method names to the mock method. This functionality can lead to some confusing results, as seen in Example 7-10, so use it with caution.

Example 7-10. Mocking a concrete class with preserved methods

```
unit_tests do
    test "that using a Java class in JRuby string calls toString" do
        preservedMethods = ['size', JtestR::Mocha::METHODS_TO_LEAVE_ALONE].flatten

        list = mock(java.util.ArrayList, preservedMethods)

        list.expects(:add).times(2).returns(true)

        assert list.size == 0

        list.add "one"
        list.add "two"

        assert list.size == 0 # this is zero because the add method is mocked
    end
end
```

See Also

- Mocha website, *http://mocha.rubyforge.org/*

7.6 Modifying the JtestR Classpath

Problem

You need to test classes that are not available on JtestR's default classpath. By default, JtestR's classpath includes the following directories:

- *build/classes*
- *build/test_classes*
- *target/classes*
- *target/test_classes*

The default classpath also includes all JAR files in the *lib* and *build_lib* directories (and any subdirectories).

Solution

Use the JtestR configuration file, by default named *jtestr_config.rb* and placed in the *test* directory, to define the correct classpath. For example, to set the classpath to be the *bin* directory, your configuration file would contain:

```
classpath 'bin'
```

Multiple classpath definitions can be included in the configuration file.

Discussion

Using the `classpath` configuration option as described above will overwrite the default classpath. To add the default entries back, put this line to your configuration file:

```
add_common_classpath true
```

7.7 Grouping Tests for JtestR

Problem

You have a number of tests run through JtestR and want to group them.

Solution

Follow JtestR's directory naming conventions to group your tests. Within the main test directory, JtestR will automatically group your tests based on the directory they are in and will execute these groups in a particular order:

1. Unit tests, those in the *unit* directory.
2. Functional tests, those in the *functional* directory.
3. Integration tests, those in the *integration* directory.
4. Other tests, those that are not in the *unit*, *functional*, or *integration* directories.

The tests within each of these directory-based groups are then further grouped based on the testing framework used. When you run the test runner and have tests in multiple groups, you will see the test results grouped:

```
Unit TestUnit: 4 test, 0 failures, 0 errors
Integration TestUnit: 2 test, 0 failures, 0 errors
```

Here we see that there were four tests in the *unit* directory and two tests in the *integration* directory, all of which used Test/Unit.

Discussion

Although JtestR provides these automatic directory-based groups, there is nothing actually different about the environment under which unit tests run as compared with functional or integration tests.

7.8 Using the JtestR Command-Line Options

Problem

You want to customize the behavior of the JtestR command-line test runner in some way, such as limiting the tests to be run or enabling additional logging.

Solution

The JtestR command-line test runner has a number of options that can be configured through command-line arguments. Unfortunately these arguments must be passed in a specific sequence that you must adhere to:

port
> This argument, which defaults to 22332, allows you to connect the test runner to a long-lived server process. This reduces the amount of time required to perform a test run. This capability is discussed in Recipe 7.8.

tests
> This argument, which defaults to test, specifies the top-level directory in which test group directories can be found.

logging
> This argument specifies the logging level for JtestR. Possible values are NONE, ERR, WARN, INFO, and DEBUG. The default is WARN.

configFile
> This argument specifies the filename of the JtestR configuration file.

outputLevel
> This argument specifies how much information about each test is output. Possible values are NONE, QUIET, NORMAL, VERBOSE, and DEFAULT.

output
> This argument provides JtestR with the output location. The default is STDOUT.

groups
> This argument defines the test group (or groups, in which case they should be comma-delimited) that will be run. The default is to run all tests discovered.

One typical use of these arguments is to output the name of each test as it is run. As you can see from the output above, by default, JtestR only outputs an individual test name if something goes wrong. By setting the outputLevel argument to VERBOSE, you can have it output each test name:

```
$ java org.jtestr.JtestRRunner 22332 test WARN jtsetr_config.rb VERBOSE
test_that_empty_works(TestArrayList): .
test_that_size_method_works(TestArrayList): .
Unit TestUnit: 1 test, 0 failures, 0 errors
```

See Also

- Recipe 7.7, "Grouping Tests for JtestR"
- Recipe 7.11, "Improving JtestR Performance"

7.9 Running JtestR with Ant

Problem

You are building a project with Apache Ant and want to add tests written in Ruby.

Solution

Use the Ant task provided with JtestR. This can be done by adding the following task definition to your Ant *build.xml* file:

```
<taskdef name="jtestr"
    classname="org.jtestr.ant.JtestRAntRunner" classpath="lib/jtestr-0.3.jar" />
```

Then call this task from inside an Ant target:

```
<target name="test">
    <jtestr />
</target>
```

This target can then be run from the command line:

```
$ ant test
```

Discussion

The JtestR Ant task supports all of the options used by the command-line test runner (see Recipe 7.8). For example, to turn on verbose output, your target would look like this:

```
<target name="test">
    <jtestr outputLevel="VERBOSE" />
</target>
```

In addition to the command-line options, there is a `failOnError` option that defaults to `true`. Use this option if you want the Ant build to continue even if the tests fail.

See Also

- Ant website, *http://ant.apache.org/*
- Recipe 7.6, "Modifying the JtestR Classpath"
- Recipe 7.11, "Improving JtestR Performance"

7.10 Running JtestR with Maven

Problem

You are building a project with Maven and want to add tests written in Ruby.

Solution

Use the Maven plugin provided with JtestR. This can be done by adding the following plugin reference to your *pom.xml* file:

```
<plugin>
    <groupId>org.jtestr</groupId>
    <artifactId>jtestr</artifactId>
    <version>0.3</version>
    <executions>
        <execution>
            <goals>
                <goal>test</goal>
            </goals>
        </execution>
    </executions>
</plugin>
```

Once this is in place, JtestR will automatically run whenever Maven's test phase is executed.

Unfortunately, the latest release (0.3) of JtestR's Maven support has a dependency on a nonstandard JRuby library. As a result, when you try to use the plugin, you may see this error:

```
[ERROR] BUILD ERROR
[INFO] ------------------------------------------------------------
[INFO] Failed to resolve artifact.

Missing:
----------
1) org.jruby:jruby-complete:jar:r6947

  Try downloading the file manually from the project website.
...
----------
1 required artifact is missing.

for artifact:
  org.jtestr:jtestr:maven-plugin:0.3
```

To correct this, download the JAR from *http://dist.codehaus.org/jtestr/jruby-complete -r6947.jar* and install it into your local Maven repository. This can be done with these commands:

```
$ wget http://dist.codehaus.org/jtestr/jruby-complete-r6947.jar
$ mvn install:install-file -Dfile=jruby-complete-r6947.jar -Dversion=r6947 \
  -DartifactId=jruby-complete -Dpackaging=jar -DgroupId=org.jruby
```

Discussion

The JtestR Maven plugin supports all of the options used by the command-line test runner (see Recipe 7.7). For example, to only run unit tests, your plugin configuration would look like this:

```
<plugin>
    <groupId>org.jtestr</groupId>
    <artifactId>jtestr</artifactId>
    <version>0.3</version>
    <executions>
        <execution>
            <goals>
                <goal>test</goal>
            </goals>
        </execution>
    </executions>
    <configuration>
        <groups>Unit TestUnit</groups>
    </configuration>
</plugin>
```

In addition to the command-line options, there is a `failOnError` option that defaults to true. Use this option if you want the build to continue even if the tests fail.

See Also

- Maven website, *http://maven.apache.org/*
- Recipe 7.6, "Modifying the JtestR Classpath"
- Recipe 7.11, "Improving JtestR Performance"

7.11 Improving JtestR Performance

Problem

You are using JtestR and want to accelerate the execution times of your unit tests.

Solution

Start a JtestR server in the background. This can be done with the class `org.jtestr.Back groundServer`:

```
$ java org.jtestr.BackgroundServer
```

By default, this will create a server on port 22332 with two runtimes, meaning that two sets of tests can be run simultaneously. To change these options, you can use command-line arguments: the port followed by the number of runtimes. For example, to start five runtimes listening on port 1000 you would run:

```
$ java org.jtestr.BackgroundServer 1000 5
```

Note that if you deviate from the default port, you will need to specify this when you start the test runner. For example, with the command-line test runner, this is the first option:

```
$ java org.jtestr.JtestRRunner 1000
```

Discussion

JtestR also includes classes that allow this test server to be run from inside an Ant or Maven build. For Ant, this is done with the **JtestRAntServer** class:

```
<target name="server">
  <taskdef name="jtestr-server"
    classname="org.jtestr.ant.JtestRAntServer" classpath="lib/jtestr-0.3.jar" />
  <jtestr-server />
</target>
```

For Maven, if you have the JtestR Maven plugin configured in your *pom.xml*, you can start the server by running this on the command line:

```
$ mvn jtestr:server
```

See Also

- Recipe 7.9, "Running JtestR with Ant"
- Recipe 7.10, "Running JtestR with Maven"

## CHAPTER 8

The JRuby Community

8.0 Introduction

This final chapter includes a series of recipes about how to participate in the JRuby community. First, we will look at building JRuby from source, something that most developers looking to peek under the covers of JRuby will need to do at some point. We will also do a quick walkthrough of JRuby's issue management system before finishing up with some information about the ways in which JRuby community members communicate with each other.

8.1 Building JRuby from Source

Problem

You need to build JRuby from the source files. This could be to take advantage of some unreleased code or to create a JRuby JAR file for distribution.

Solution

Download the source using a Subversion client:

```
$ svn co http://svn.codehaus.org/jruby/trunk/jruby/
```

JRuby is built using Apache Ant. There are a number of useful Ant targets in the provided build script:

jar
> Creates the *jruby.jar* file.

jar-complete
> Creates the *jruby-complete.jar* file, which includes all of the contents from *jruby.jar* and all of the Ruby standard libraries.

test
> Runs the JRuby unit test suite.

`dist-bin`
> Creates the JRuby binary distribution, i.e., the ZIP file that you download from *http://dist.codehaus.org/jruby/*.

Discussion

The Subversion command above will check out the most recent version of the source code (the trunk) from the JRuby repository. However, some times it is necessary to check out the source core that corresponds to a release. This can be done by checking out one of the tags under *http://svn.codehaus.org/jruby/tags/*. For example, the source of the JRuby 1.1 release can be found at *http://svn.codehaus.org/jruby/tags/jruby-1_1/*.

The Ant script also includes two targets that relate to JRuby's compatibility with other Ruby interpreters. Although there is no formal language specification for Ruby, a wide-ranging test suite has been created as part of the Rubinius project. JRuby's Ant script includes the following targets that relate to these specifications:

`spec`
> Test all of the released specifications that JRuby is known to be able to pass.

`spec-all`
> Test all of the released Ruby specifications.

`spec-show-excludes`
> List the specifications that JRuby is known to not be able to pass.

`spec-latest`
> Test all of the available Ruby specifications that JRuby is known to be able to pass, first obtaining the specification files from source control.

`spec-latest-all`
> Test all of the available Ruby specifications, first obtaining the specification files from source control.

See Also

- Rubinius specs documentation, *http://rubinius.lighthouseapp.com/projects/5089/the-rubinius-specs*

8.2 Submitting an Issue Report for JRuby

Problem

You have discovered a problem with JRuby or wish to request a feature to be added in a future version.

Solution

JRuby uses Atlassian JIRA as its issue-tracking tool. You can view the list of issues and create new issue reports by going to *http://jira.codehaus.org/browse/JRUBY*. You can browse issues anonymously, but must register and log in before creating a new issue or commenting on an existing issue. Before creating an issue, please search previously submitted issues to avoid duplication.

Assuming you want to create an issue and have logged in, click the Create New Issue link in the main navigation to start the issue creation process. Figure 8-1 shows the resulting dialog.

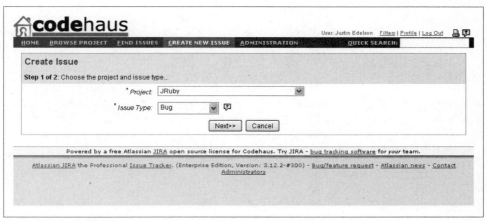

Figure 8-1. JIRA Create Issue dialog

Once you have selected the appropriate issue type and clicked Next, you should populate the following form with as much information as possible. This will assist JRuby developers in fully understanding the issue.

Discussion

At the bottom of the Issue Details form are two form fields, seen in Figure 8-2, that provide you with an opportunity to prioritize the handling of your issue.

Figure 8-2. Testcase and Patch form fields

The first, "Testcase included," allows you to specify that you have attached (or will attach) a test that demonstrates the issue in a repeatable manner. The ability to reliably reproduce an issue is vital to resolving it. The second, "Patch Submitted," allows you to specify that you have attached (or will attach) a patch to the JRuby source that resolves the issue. It is common to create a patch against the latest source from version control, not the most recent release.

See Also

- Recipe 8.3, "Using the JRuby Mailing Lists"

8.3 Using the JRuby Mailing Lists

Problem

You need assistance with JRuby or a related tool.

Solution

Subscribe to the JRuby User mailing list. Subscriptions are managed through Xircles, a project management system developed for use by the Codehaus. You can see the available JRuby mailing lists by going to *http://xircles.codehaus.org/projects/jruby/lists*. A searchable archive of the mailing list is also available on this page.

Discussion

In addition to the mailing lists, JRuby core developers can frequently be found in the #jruby IRC channel on *irc.freenode.net*. Conversations on this channel are logged and an archive is available through *http://codingbitch.com/irc/channel?channel=%23jruby*.

Index

We'd like to hear your suggestions for improving our indexes. Send email to *index@oreilly.com*.

About the Authors

Justin Edelson is the vice president of Platform Engineering for MTV Networks. He was the coauthor (with Brett McLaughlin) of *Java & XML*, Third Edition (O'Reilly), published in December, 2006.

Henry Liu is an experienced software developer and game designer. He is currently a senior software developer at MTV Networks. He maintains an open source Ruby project for collaborative filtering named slopeone-gem and is an active member of the New York City Ruby Users Group.

Colophon

The animal on the cover of *JRuby Cookbook* is an African civet (*Civettictis civetta*). Unlike the other members of the Viverridae family, which resemble cats, the African civet is a dog-like animal with large hindquarters and a low-head stance. Its coat is gray with black stripes and spots, and it has a gray face, a white snout, and dark markings around its eyes like a raccoon. Along its back runs a short mane of stiff hairs that stand on end when the civet is alarmed. From head to tail, an African civet is about 4 feet long, and it weighs 30 to 40 pounds.

The African civet ranges across sub-Saharan Africa in forests and savannas. Solitary and nocturnal, it hides in caves or tree hollows during the day. It eats anything edible, including insects, plants, and carrion, and it preys on small animals such as hares and moongooses. Like all civets, the African civet has glands that produce a scented fluid, which it uses to mark its territory. This musk, known as civetone or simply civet, is one of the oldest known ingredients in perfumes. Although it is still used in the perfume industry today, the trade for civet musk has been on the decline since synthetic musk was introduced in the mid-1900s.

The cover image is from Richard Lydekker's *Royal Natural History*. The cover font is Adobe ITC Garamond. The text font is Linotype Birka; the heading font is Adobe Myriad Condensed; and the code font is LucasFont's TheSansMonoCondensed.

The O'Reilly Advantage

Stay Current and Save Money